W9-BVT-445

RELATIVISM:
A GUIDE FOR THE PERPLEXED

Continuum *Guides for the Perplexed*

Continuum's Guides for the Perplexed are clear, concise and accessible introductions to thinkers, writers and subjects that students and readers can find especially challenging. Concentrating specifically on what it is that makes the subject difficult to grasp, these books explain and explore key themes and ideas, guiding the reader towards a thorough understanding of demanding material.

Guides for the Perplexed available from Continuum:

Adorno: A Guide for the Perplexed, Alex Thomson
Deleuze: A Guide for the Perplexed, Claire Colebrook
Derrida: A Guide for the Perplexed, Julian Wolfreys
Descartes: A Guide for the Perplexed, Justin Skirry
Existentialism: A Guide for the Perplexed, Stephen Earnshaw
Freud: A Guide for the Perplexed, Céline Surprenant
Gadamer: A Guide for the Perplexed, Chris Lawn
Habermas: A Guide for the Perplexed, Eduardo Mendieta
Hegel: A Guide for the Perplexed, David James
Hobbes: A Guide for the Perplexed, Stephen J. Finn
Hume: A Guide for the Perplexed, Angela Coventry
Husserl: A Guide for the Perplexed, Matheson Russell
Kant: A Guide for the Perplexed, T. K. Seung
Kierkegaard: A Guide for the Perplexed, Clare Carlisle
Leibniz: A Guide for the Perplexed, Franklin Perkins
Levinas: A Guide for the Perplexed, B. C. Hutchens
Merleau-Ponty: A Guide for the Perplexed, Eric Matthews
Nietzsche: A Guide for the Perplexed, R. Kevin Hill
Plato: A Guide for the Perplexed, Gerald A. Press
Quine: A Guide for the Perplexed, Gary Kemp
Ricoeur: A Guide for the Perplexed, David Pellauer
Rousseau: A Guide for the Perplexed, Matthew Simpson
Sartre: A Guide for the Perplexed, Gary Cox
Spinoza: A Guide for the Perplexed, Charles Jarrett
Wittgenstein: A Guide for the Perplexed, Mark Addis

RELATIVISM: A GUIDE FOR THE PERPLEXED

TIMOTHY MOSTELLER

continuum

Continuum

Continuum International Publishing Group
The Tower Building   80 Maiden Lane
11 York Road   Suite 704
London SE1 7NX   New York NY 10038

British Library Cataloguing-in-Publication Data
A catalogue record for this book is available from the British Library.

ISBN-10: HB: 0-8264-9699-7
PB: 0-8264-9700-4
ISBN-13: HB: 978-0-8264-9699-7
PB: 978-0-8264-9700-0

Library of Congress Cataloging-in-Publication Data
Mosteller, Timothy,
Relativism : a guide for the perplexed / (p.   ) and index.
ISBN 978-0-8264-9699-7 – ISBN 978-0-8264-9700-0 1. Relativity. I. Title.
BD221.M665   2008
149–dc22
2007042372

Typeset by Servis Filmsetting Ltd, Manchester
Printed and bound in Great Britain by
MPG Books, Ltd, Bodmin, Cornwall

CONTENTS

To my mother and father, with love.

ACKNOWLEDGEMENTS

I am grateful to the administration at California Baptist University for travel funding for participation in several academic conferences in which ideas for this manuscript were explored. Special thanks is due to Cornerstone University, the University of Central Florida and London Metropolitan University for hosting quality conferences where I was able to present papers on the topics of relativism and its connection with issues in religion, politics and philosophy. I am also grateful for my students who ask the hard and probing questions about the limit, scope and extent of human knowledge and the challenge that relativism plays in developing an overall philosophy for one's life. Thanks is due as well to Aaron Preston, Kevin Timpe and Dallas Willard for providing helpful suggestions for the manuscript.

CHAPTER 1

A DEFINITION AND BRIEF HISTORY OF RELATIVISM

INTRODUCTION

Relativism is a multi-faceted topic that ranges over a vast array of areas of human enquiry, from pop culture to technical journals in philosophy. In discussions of relativism, one often hears cited Allan Bloom's famous quotation from his controversial work *The Closing of the American Mind*, that, 'There is one thing a professor can be absolutely sure of; almost every student entering the university believes, or says he believes, that truth is relative' (Bloom 1987, p. 25).

There appears to be some empirical data that may support Bloom's claim. For example, consider the following:

In two national surveys conducted by Barna Research, one among adults and one among teenagers, people were asked if they believe that there are moral absolutes that are unchanging or that moral truth is relative to the circumstances. By a 3-to-1 margin (64% vs. 22%) adults said truth is always relative to the person and their situation. The perspective was even more lop-sided among teenagers, 83% of whom said moral truth depends on the circumstances, and only 6% of whom said moral truth is absolute (Barna Group 2002).

This may not mean that a majority of Americans are moral relativists in a strong sense, but it does give some support for the idea that relativism is part of how people think about philosophical issues today.[1]

Whether unreflective relativism is a default intellectual position in contemporary Western culture remains to be seen. This guide is not meant as a proof that relativism is accepted by most people; rather this study will attempt to show what relativism is and the various criticisms of it that occur in the sub-disciplines of philosophy. We begin this chapter with a short discussion of how to define and understand relativism broadly speaking. We then present a brief survey of the history of relativistic thought. We conclude this chapter with a cautionary note that seeks to be charitable to some forms of relativistic thought while simultaneously maintaining that certain forms of relativism are intellectually implausible.

DEFINING RELATIVISM

What is relativism?[2] In developing a general statement of what relativism is, it may be useful to examine several recent definitions of relativism. Consider the following: 'Any doctrine could be called relativism which holds that something exists, or has certain properties or features, or is true or in some sense obtains, not simply but only in relation to something else' (Lacey 1986, p. 206). This definition is too broad. Its broadness lies in the phrase 'only in relation to something else'. For example, philosophers who maintain some kind of correspondence theory of truth might claim that a proposition p is true in virtue of the relation that p has to a fact f; p is true only in relation to f. A theistic philosopher might argue that the universe exists and has the properties it has 'only in relation to' the mind of God. This definition will not work since 'only in relation to' includes, in the two examples just presented, alethic (truth) and ontological (existence) dependence (which is a relation of something with something else) in the definition. But this is not what is ordinarily meant by advocates of relativism. There are only certain kinds of relations that result in relativism.

Other definitions are too narrow. For example: 'Relativism [is] the denial that there are certain kinds of universal truths' (Pojman 1995, p. 690). This definition puts an epistemic premium on what relativism is, but not all forms of relativism need to have epistemic elements – although all forms of relativism have epistemic implications. Ontological relativism, according to which the existence and/or nature of some entity x is relative to language(s), concepts, etc., does not seem to have an epistemic element to it. However, it seems to have epistemic implications in that if the existence and/or nature of an entity x is relative to language, then knowing that x exists and exists as such, will be dependent upon what x is like which is dependent upon language, concepts or whatever.

Let me propose the following definition of relativism that is broad enough to encompass a wide variety of relativism and narrow enough to exclude other varieties:

Relativism = df:
the nature and existence of items of knowledge, qualities, values or logical entities non-trivially obtain their natures and/or existence from certain aspects of human activity, including, but not limited to, beliefs, cultures, languages, etc.

This definition is broad enough to show that philosophical relativism can be applied to a variety of views within the academic discipline of philosophy (e.g. ontology, epistemology, ethics, aesthetics), but it is also narrow enough to draw out the idea that the existence of things within these philosophical categories is dependent in some non-trivial way on the activity of at least one human mind. With this notion of relativism in mind, let us turn briefly to examine a short history of relativistic thought in Western philosophy.

A BRIEF HISTORY OF RELATIVISM[3]

From the history of philosophy, it appears that the first articulation of relativism (at least in its epistemic form) was given by Protagoras in his work *Truth*, now lost but most widely known through Plato's presentation of it in the *Theaetetus*. What exactly is Protagorean relativism? It is simply the view that 'what seems true to anyone is true for him to whom it seems so' (Plato, *Theaetetus* 170a). Siegel claims,

Protagoras' view is an extreme version of relativism: knowledge and truth are relative to the person contemplating the proposition in question. p is true (for me) if it so seems; false (for me) if it so seems. Since the final arbiter of truth and knowledge is the individual, Protagoras' view denies the existence of any standard or criterion higher than the individual by which claims to truth and knowledge can be adjudicated (Siegel 1987, p. 4).

Harré and Krausz also recognize that Protagorean relativism is extreme in its formulation. Part of what makes Protagorean relativism extreme lies in the making of knowledge relative to the individual. Harré and Krausz concur with Siegel when they state,

> Protagorean relativism is an extreme form of truth relativism. It is extreme in the sense that it makes the truth or warranted assertibility of propositions relative to individual persons on unique occasions. This is a most implausible doctrine, in that we could hardly imagine a coherent form of life developing in such circumstances. But there are other varieties of epistemic relativism which are not so easily dismissed. One could concede the possibility that every general relativism holds among large scale belief systems without embracing extreme Protagorean individualism (Harré and Krausz 1996, p. 74).

As Harré and Krausz recognize, the extreme individualism makes Protagorean relativism problematic.[4]

Although relativism has its philosophical beginning with Protagoras, it has been present in various ways and in various times throughout the long history of Western thought from the 'pre-Socratic' period up through the 21st century. However, one is hard pressed to find hints of relativism in post-Aristotelian philosophy, Roman philosophy and early Christian philosophy, or even find philosophers being accused of holding to relativistic thought, until the 16th century. While the Romans had their sceptics, they did not seem to have their relativists, and with the rise of the 'church age' in the Middle Ages, given the canonical theism so dominant in this period, there was no room for relativism of any kind.

It was not until the Renaissance that relativism appears once again to provide a challenge to the thought of classical antiquity and the medieval synthesis of faith and reason. The historian of philosophy Fredrick Copleston accuses the Renaissance philosopher Michel de Montaigne (1533–92) of reviving in his essays 'the ancient arguments for . . . the relativity of sense-experience, the impossibility of the intellect's rising above this relativity to the sure attainment of absolute truth . . . [and] the relativity of value judgments' (Copleston 1993, p. 228).

Probably the most famous Enlightenment philosopher holding to, or at least accused of holding to, a form of relativism was Giambattista Vico (1688–1744). Vico (most famous for his views about the nature of history) developed an epistemology in which truth is understood as something that is made. Vico states, 'it is reasonable to assume that the ancient sages of Italy entertained the following beliefs about the true. "The true is precisely what is made"', and 'human truth is what man puts together and makes in the act of knowing it' (Vico 1988, p. 46). This sounds like it could lead to a form of relativism with respect to truth being made by particular individuals or groups of individuals. However, Vico was not a wholescale relativist. He did not believe that our knowledge of the physical world was relative to the human mind, but only that our knowledge of geometrical and mathematical objects is created by the mind. His view was that we come to have 'scientific knowledge of Nature only in so far as we remake, as it were the structure of the object in the cognitive order' (Copleston 1993, p. 156). Vico was also not a relativist with regard to the goodness or badness of particular customs in history. He did not claim like the Greek sceptics 'that it is impossible to judge whether one custom is better or worse than another' (Burke 1985, p. 56). We will look at some 20th-century examples of wholescale ethical relativism in Chapter 3.

Other philosophers from the 17th and 18th centuries, such as Charles de Secondat Montesquieu (1689–1755), François Marie Arouet de Voltaire (1694–1778) and Johann Gottfried Herder (1744–1803), like Vico claimed that things appeared relativistic, but were merely partial relativists. For example, Voltaire pointed out the differences in moral views across cultures, but he rejected 'extreme ethical relativism' (Copleston 1993, p. 23).

In the 18th and 19th centuries, proponents of relativism seem to begin to sprout up both in Great Britain and on the Continent. Sir William Hamilton (1788–1856) in a section of his works entitled the 'Relativity of Human Knowledge' states, 'We must, therefore, more precisely limit our sphere of knowledge, by adding, that all we know is known only under the special conditions of our faculties. "Man," says Protagoras, "is the measure of the universe"' (Hamilton 1861, p. 91). Hamilton follows with a lengthy quotation from Bacon, 'All perceptions, as well of the senses as of the mind, are conformed to the nature of the percipient individual, and not to the true nature of the universe which distorts and discolours the nature of things, by mingling its own nature with it' (p. 92). Hamilton appears to be arguing that perceptual knowledge is relative to the individual. He states, 'In the perception of an external object, the mind does not know it in immediate relation to itself, but mediately, in relation to the material organs of sense' (p. 94).

It is not clear to what extent Hamilton maintains relativism about knowledge, as it appears that he is simply arguing that knowledge comes from perception and our perceptions of objects are relative to our sense faculties and the physiological apparatus through which we sense things. However, his invocation of Protagoras is non-trivial. If Protagorean relativism amounts to a self-refuting position and Hamilton is invoking these Protagorean views as predecessors of his own, then his own views will succumb to these difficulties as well. While it is not my task here to evaluate Hamilton's views, it is historically noteworthy that Hamilton is one of the figures in the history of philosophy who holds to a form of relativism that lay dormant for millennia.

In a commentary of Hamilton's work, John Stuart Mill praises Hamilton stating, 'Among the philosophical writers of the present century in these islands, no one occupies a higher position than Sir William Hamilton' (Mill 1866, p. 9). However, Mill recognized that the notion of the relativity of knowledge is not without difficulties. The person claiming that knowledge is relative in the sense that

> we may . . . be looking at Things in themselves, but through imperfect glasses: that we see may be the very Thing, but the colours and forms which the glass conveys to us may be partly an optical illusion . . . could not, consistently, assert that all our knowledge is relative; since his opinion would be that we have a capacity of Absolute knowledge, but that we are liable to mistake relative knowledge for it (p. 27).

Mill concludes after his examination of Hamilton's views that it does not appear that Hamilton held to the relativity of knowledge in any but a trivial sense in which 'we can only know what we can know' (p. 40) which, according to Mill, is a 'barren truism' (p. 41).

Turning now to the 19th century, we find that the philosopher Augustus Comte (1798–1857) is also accused of relativism. Wilhelm Windelband, in his *A History of Philosophy*, states:

> Comte's projected positive system of the sciences first of all pushes Hume's and Condillac's conception to the farthest point. Not only is human knowledge assigned for its province to the reciprocal

relations of phenomena, but there is nothing absolute whatever, that might lie unknown, as it were, at the basis of phenomena. The only absolute principle is, that all is relative. To talk of first causes of ultimate ends of things has no rational sense (Windelband 1901, pp. 650–1).

Similarly, Herbert Spencer (1820–1903) in his *First Principles* following in Hamilton's path, maintains that knowledge is relative (Spencer 1958, pp. 80–1). At the close of the 19th century, Friedrich Wilhelm Nietzsche (1844–1900) is saddled by Copleston with a strong view of relativism. Copleston states:

But there is, according to Nietzsche, no absolute truth. The concept of absolute truth is an invention of philosophers who are dissatisfied with the world of Becoming and seek an abiding world of Being. 'Truth is that sort of error without which a particular type of living being could not live. The value for life is ultimately decisive' (Copleston 1993, p. 409).[5]

The obvious comment on Nietzsche's general view of truth is that it presupposes the possibility of occupying an absolute standpoint from which the relativity of all truth or its fictional character can be asserted, and that this presupposition is at variance with the relativist interpretation of truth. Further, this comment by no means loses its point if Nietzsche is willing to say that his own view of truth is perspectival and 'fictional'. No doubt Nietzsche would admit this in principle, while insisting that his interpretation of the world was the expression of a higher form of the Will to Power. But what is the standard of higher or lower (p. 410)? With the advent of the 20th century, Ferdinand Canning Scott Schiller (1864–1937) raises the banner of relativism in a way that is unprecedented in the history of philosophy to this point. Schiller states that Protagoras' 'famous dictum that "man is the measure of all things" must be ranked even above the Delphic "Know thyself," as compressing the largest quantum of vital meaning into the most compact form' (Schiller 1912, p. 33). Schiller criticizes the Platonic (ultimately an 'idealist') notion of a duplication of the real world with the Ideal world. Schiller maintains contra Plato that concepts are not eternal, timeless entities by means of which we know through grasping them with our intellect. Rather, concepts are not unalterable and only relatively constant (like mere material things), being essentially tools slowly fashioned by a practical intelligence for the mastery of its experience, whose value and truth reside in their application to the particular cases of their use, and not in their timeless validity nor in their supra sensible otium cum dignitate in a transcendent realm of abstractions (p. 64).

Regarding truth and rationality Schiller urges,

Let us go back to Plato, by all means; but let us go back not with the intention of repeating his mistake and painfully plunging into the 'chasm' he has made, but in order to correct his initial error. But to do this we must return from Plato to Protagoras. We must abandon the attempt to dehumanize knowledge, to attribute to it an 'independence' of human purposes, an 'absoluteness' which divorces it from life, an 'eternity' of truth must mean its applicability at whatever time we will . . . we must start once more, with Protagoras (p. 69).

In a little fictional dialogue entitled 'Protagoras the Humanist' Schiller forms a conversation between Protagoras and a philosopher named Morosophus. Schiller has Protagoras discuss how we 'make' the world into what it is. He states, 'We "find" a world made for us, because we are the heirs of bygone ages, profiting by their work, and it may be suffering for their folly. But we can in part remake it, and reform a world that has slowly formed itself. But of all this how could we get an inkling if we had not begun by perceiving that of all things, Man, each man, is the measure' (p. 320). Although Nelson Goodman does not acknowledge Schiller in his little book, the title alone, *Ways of Worldmaking*, would probably have made Schiller quite happy.[6]

It is not my purpose here to give an entire history of relativism. Nor is it my task to speculate as to why relativism is largely absent from the philosophical scene for nearly 2,000 years. Rather it is simply my intent to place current discussions of relativism in a bit of historical context preceding our own times that one philosopher speculates will be called 'The Age of Relativism' (Harris 1992, p. 1). Philosophical views usually have some historical roots, and relativism as it appears in contemporary philosophy is no exception.

Just as philosophers in the past have examined other philosophers' works, examining the putatively relativistic claims that are made by various philosophers (Plato vs. Protagoras; Mill vs. Hamilton; Copleston vs. Nietzsche), so too it is our task to examine the relativistic claims made in our own time to see what we can learn from these claims and what we must reject. We turn now to that task with a look at relativism in the three main areas of philosophy: epistemology, ontology, ethics and aesthetics.

A CAUTIONARY NOTE

Relativism in philosophy and in other disciplines has become so much of a concern it has sparked an understandable backlash. Relativism is often raised as a bugbear to motivate people to reject a certain position or cluster of positions in philosophy that lead to an 'anything goes' view of the particular topic under discussion, especially in ethics.[7] While the bulk of this particular work aims to show the problems of relativistic thinking in various areas of philosophical enquiry, and is thus anti-relativistic, I want to be careful at the outset to recognize that anti-relativistic thought is often used to justify positions which, while not relativistic, are certainly not entailed by a failure of relativism. For example, while it may be the case that relativistic thought in ontology fails, this does not entail Platonic dualism about reality; epistemological relativism, while self-defeating, does not entail either a correspondence or coherence view of truth; relativism in ethics might be incoherent, but this does not entail that an Aristotelian virtue theory is the way in which we ought to approach the good life; relativism in religion may be intellectually implausible, but this entails neither theism nor atheism. The bulk of the arguments in each chapter of this book focus on the main difficulties faced by a particular philosophical outlook, namely a relativistic one. So, while this book is anti-relativistic, I am aware that anti-anti-relativism might not be such a bad position as well, especially if the anti-relativism in question is used to support philosophical views that it is unable to support.

Clifford Geertz in a very readable essay sketches the possibly false dichotomy between relativism and anti-relativism. Geertz writes:

We are being offered a choice of worries. What the relativists, so-called, want us to worry about is provincialism – the danger that our perceptions will be dulled, our intellects constricted, and our sympathies narrowed by the overlearned and overvalued acceptances of our own society. What the antirelativists, self-declared, want us to worry about, and worry about and worry about, as though our very souls depended upon it, is a kind of spiritual entropy, a heat death of the mind, in which everything is as significant, thus as insignificant, as everything else: anything goes, to each his own, you pays your money and you takes your choice, I know what I like, not in the south, *tout comprendre, c'est tout pardonner* (Geertz 1984, p. 265).

Geertz' reminder here is a good one. Although Geertz' paper takes place within the context of the discipline of anthropology, relativistic views in philosophy are related to these ideas. On the one hand, relativistic philosophical tendencies may have the virtues which Geertz points out such as warning us against provincialism. On the other hand, anti-relativistic philosophical positions rightly warn us about the 'anything goes' attitudes that seem to arise from relativism.

However, Geertz claims that some thinkers (e.g. Paul Johnson in *Modern Times*) maintain that 'Cultural Relativism causes everything bad' (p. 267). Cultural relativism is not the root of all evil. False beliefs, wrong accounts of reality, moral evils can be easily had without relativism. Geertz is an anti-relativist *and* an anti-anti-relativist. I am sympathetic to this position. Thus, although this book will argue against relativism, this does not imply that relativism as such is the root of all evil. It most certainly is not, even though it is implausible as an approach to philosophical inquiry.

CHAPTER 2

EPISTEMOLOGICAL RELATIVISM[1]

INTRODUCTION

Epistemological relativism (ER) shows up in some of the most rigorous philosophical works published by some of the best university presses in the world[2] and in ordinary conversation or 'debates' on talk radio shows where a caller might say to a host, 'Well that's true for you, but not true for me!' This sort of 'man on the street' locution is symptomatic of relativism in the broader culture, and is an instance of the more nuanced forms of epistemic relativism in contemporary philosophy. In this chapter we will accomplish three things. First, we will define epistemological relativism and analyse its main features. Second, we will examine some of the types of argument that are put forward in *favour* of relativism in the epistemic sense and examine their main weaknesses. Third, we will examine two of the main arguments *against* relativism: 1) it is self-defeating and 2) it leads to solipsism. This will be followed by some of the responses by relativists against these two types of argument, and I will argue that these relativistic responses are unsatisfactory.

WHAT IS EPISTEMOLOGICAL RELATIVISM?

Harvey Siegel's account of ER gives us a nice starting point for an analysis of this philosophical position. Siegel defines epistemological relativism in the following two-part fashion. First, there is a 'standards' conjunct, which states:

For any knowledge-claim p, p can be evaluated (assessed, established, etc.) only according to (with reference to) one or another set of background principles and standards of evaluation $s_1, \ldots s_n$.

Second, there is a 'no neutrality' conjunct which states:

and, given a different set (or sets) of background principles and standards $s_1', \ldots s_n'$, there is no neutral (that is, neutral with respect to the two (or more) alternative sets of principles and standards) way of choosing between the two (or more) alternative sets in evaluating p with respect to truth or rational justification. p's truth and rational justifiability are relative to the standards used in evaluating p (Siegel 1987, p. 6).

The key element of Siegel's definition is the notion of there being no neutral (i.e. non-question begging) standard(s) by means of which to determine the 'truth or rational justification' of any knowledge claim. Siegel's definition is particularly helpful in that it does not specify any particular standard, but leaves room for the application of any standard whatsoever.[3]

ARGUMENTS FOR ER AND WHY THEY FAIL

Siegel (2004) discusses two arguments for ER, the 'no neutrality, therefore relativism' and the 'no transcendence, therefore relativism' arguments. The former begins with the assumption that there are no neutral standards between competing knowledge claims and concludes that knowledge claims are relative to whatever non-neutral framework from which that knowledge claim is made, and this argument runs as follows:

i. There are no neutral standards by appeal to which competing knowledge claims can be adjudicated.
ii. If there are no neutral standards by appeal to which competing knowledge claims can be adjudicated, then ER obtains.
iii. Therefore, ER obtains.

The key premise of this argument is premise i. Is premise i. true? According to Siegel, the relativist's use of this premise hinges on an ambiguity in the idea that there is no neutrality between competing knowledge claims. It may be the case that for any two competing knowledge claims there may not be neutral standards. There may be no neutral standards which are 'neutral with respect for all possible disputes. There may nevertheless be standards which . . . are neutral in the weaker sense that they do not unfairly prejudice any particular, live (at a time) dispute' (Siegel 2004).

Perhaps we can make the distinction between 'local' and 'global' neutrality. While it may be the case that there is no global neutrality, that is neutrality that applies to all epistemic disputes, for any particular dispute, there may be local standards to which we can appeal, standards that do not prejudice either one of the contestants in a *particular* dispute. So, premise i. could be disambiguated into the following:

i'. There are no *globally* neutral standards by appeal to which competing knowledge claims can be adjudicated.

i''. There are no *locally* neutral standards by appeal to which competing knowledge claims can be adjudicated.

If the relativist maintains i'., the anti-relativist can allow this premise while maintaining that relativism does not follow, since it may be possible to maintain that there may be local neutrality, but what if the relativist maintains i''.? Does relativism follow from the no neutrality argument listed above? Siegel offers two reasons to think that it does not. First, Siegel argues that the first premise is false. He states, 'we have as yet no reason to think that the weaker form of neutrality [local neutrality] required for the avoidance of relativism in any given [local] case cannot be had' (p. 13). In addition, Siegel points out that there are in fact locally neutral standards by means of which one can evaluate competing knowledge claims. For example, although there may be competing standards of evaluation for a particular knowledge claim, there often are some standards that are considered to be locally neutral by those parties that are making those claims, and the laws of logic often function as such locally neutral standards. However, the laws of logic themselves need not always be locally neutral, since knowledge claims about them may also be disputed. In cases where the laws of logic are being considered as true or false, one cannot appeal to the laws of logic as locally neutral arbiters in the dispute. There may in fact be competing knowledge claims about the laws of logic, in which case the laws of logic cannot function as a locally neutral standard.

However, suppose that the relativist gives very persuasive reasons to think that local neutrality cannot be had. Does relativism follow? The answer is no, and this is the second reason that Siegel offers to think that relativism as a conclusion of the 'no neutrality, therefore relativism' argument fails. The relativist's claim that there is no such thing as local neutrality is either itself a neutral claim, or it is not. If it is a locally neutral claim, then the claim is false, because it claims that there is no local neutrality. If it is not locally neutral, then there cannot be any persuasive, that is non-neutrally persuasive, reasons for asserting it, and therefore it is ineffective in argumentation for the conclusion of ER, which it seeks to establish.

In addition to the 'no neutrality, therefore relativism' argument, Siegel presents a second argument, often used by defenders of ER, the 'no transcendence, therefore relativism' argument. This argument runs as follows:

i*. One cannot transcend one's perspective (framework/paradigm/culture).
ii*. If one cannot transcend one's perspective, then ER obtains.
iii*. Therefore, ER obtains.

In a way similar to that in the 'no neutrality' argument above, the 'no transcendence' argument hinges on an ambiguity in premise i. Siegel argues that i. might be disambiguated by making a distinction between global and local perspectives.[4]

i*'. One cannot globally transcend all perspectives.
i*''. One cannot locally transcend a particular perspective.

The anti-relativist can agree with the relativist if the relativist maintains i*'. The anti-relativist can deny ER, and also maintain that for any given claim made within a perspective, it may be the case that there is no global transcendence (i.e. no perspectiveless perspective). The anti-relativist would add, however, that there are still local perspectives that can be transcended. Does ER follow if the relativist maintains i*''.? Are there counter examples which show that there do in fact exist cases of local transcendence? Siegel provides common sense evidence that shows that it is quite common to transcend locally any particular perspective (and to improve that perspective) without global transcendence. These examples include the psychological development of children transcending their local perspective of not being able to grasp the concept of fractions, locally transcending the perspective that there are not things that cannot be seen with the naked eye, and locally transcending the perspective that women should be treated as mere objects. In each case the person in the first local perspective simply moved into an improved perspective. These examples show that although 'epistemic agents always judge from some perspective or other . . . there is no reason to think that they are trapped in or bound by their perspectives such that they cannot subject them to critical scrutiny' (p. 17). Therefore, the 'no transcendence, therefore relativism' argument fails and ER does not follow. This concludes our brief survey of an outline of some of the positive arguments for ER and the main difficulties with them. We turn now to some of the main arguments against ER and examine some rejoinders to these arguments. I will argue that these rejoinders to objections to ER fail. The first argument is that ER is self-refuting. The second (and more technically difficult) argument is that ER leads to solipsism

ARGUMENTS AGAINST ER

1st Argument Against ER: It is Self-defeating

From our short history of relativism in the previous chapter, we encountered an 'extreme' individualistic form of epistemic relativism in the form of Protagorean relativism that is a species of the general formulation of epistemological relativism given above. It is simply the view that 'things are for every man what they seem to him to be' (Plato 1997, p. 189, line 170a). But what's wrong with believing this?

Siegel draws out two arguments from Socrates' criticisms of this form of relativism in the *Theaetetus*, both of which apply not only to Protagorean relativism, but at least to epistemological relativism as it is defined above, and quite possibly to relativism of any kind. First, there is the argument that 'necessarily some beliefs are false' (the NSBF argument) (Siegel 1987, p. 6). This argument can be summarized as follows:

1. If there is a standard by which ER is judged to be false, then ER is false.
2. There is a standard by which ER is judged to be false.
3. Therefore, ER is false.

What is the relativist to make of this argument? In order to avoid this conclusion, the relativist must show that premise 1. is false. In order to deny premise 1., the relativist must deny that the falsity of ER follows from its being judged to be false, but this is impossible for the relativist, since on the very nature of the definition of relativism, all propositions (including ER) are true or false just in case they are judged to be so. To deny premise 1., the relativist must deny the very thing asserted in the definition of ER namely, that truth/falsity is relative to standards. So, the relativist in maintaining that ER is true must allow that ER is false, if a standard judges it to be so.

Maria Baghramian claims that the NSBF argument is problematic because it fails to 'distinguish between agent-relativism and context-relativism' (Baghramian 2004, p. 133), where the former is simply a form of subjectivism, while the latter 'provides for an agent-independent or what may be called a "context-relative" criterion of truth and falsity' (p. 133). According to Baghramian, the NSBF argument doesn't apply to the context-relativist, because this type of relativist denies the very distinction between being right *simpliciter* and being right according to the standards of evaluation of a particular context (e.g. cultural contexts). While this may make us 'prisoners of our own culture' (p. 133), according to Baghramian, without further argument as to why this is a problem, the NSBF argument doesn't apply.

Baghramian's distinction between agent and context relativists doesn't militate against the NSBF argument. If we accept her distinction, we end up with two new arguments:

NSBF-A:

1. If there is a standard held by an individual agent by which ER is judged to be false, then ER is false.
2. There is a standard held by an individual agent by which ER is judged to be false.
3. Therefore, ER is false.

NSBF-B:

1. If there is a standard in a particular context by one or more individuals by which ER is judged to be false, then ER is false.
2. There is a standard in a particular context by one or more individuals by which ER is judged to be false.
3. Therefore, ER is false.

Both NSBF-A and NSBF-B claim that regardless of whether relativism takes the standards of epistemic evaluation to be relative to an agent's individual beliefs, or to a context in which an agent's beliefs are formed, as long as the relativist denies the possibility of neutrality between her context-relativism (or agent-relativism) and the denial of her context-relativism, then necessarily, context-relativism (or agent-relativism) will be false.

In addition to the NSBF argument, Siegel presents the argument that ER should be rejected because it 'undermines the very notion of rightness' (Siegel 1987, p. 4), the UVNR argument. This argument can be summarized as follows:

1. 'If ER is rationally justifiable, [then] there must be some non-relative, neutral . . . framework or ground from which we can make that judgement [i.e. that ER is rationally justifiable]' (p. 4).
2. But according to the definition of ER there are no non-relative, neutral frameworks or grounds.
3. Therefore, ER is not a rationally justifiable position.

The relativist must take issue with premise 1. in this argument. The relativist must claim that it is true that ER is rationally justifiable and that it is false that a neutral framework is required. However, whatever rational justification that the relativist has for the affirmation of the antecedent and the denial of the consequent of premise 1., it cannot be a justification that is itself neutral, since the relativist is seeking to deny the possibility of any such neutrality. The very notion of the rightness or truth of a proposition has been undermined in the very definition of relativism. Thus, if ER is true, it would be false, since 'there can be no neutral ground from which to assess the rational justifiability of any claim, including ER itself' (Siegel 1987, p. 8).

Using Siegel's understanding of ER, it is also possible to show that ER leads to a *reductio ad absurdum*. Consider the following:

1. If ER is a 'rationally justifiable position', then 'there are good reasons for holding ER' (Siegel 1987, p. 8).
2. If there are good reasons for holding ER, then those good reasons are neutral (by definition of 'good reason').
3. According to the proponent of ER, it is not the case that those good reasons are neutral.

4. Therefore, according to the proponent of ER, there are not good reasons for holding ER.
5. Therefore, according to the proponent of ER, ER is not a rationally justifiable position.

The focal point of this argument is the truth value of premise 2. The notion of neutrality required for this argument to work is one according to which the good reasons for holding to ER are neutral 'with respect to the presuppositions of relativists and non-relativists' (p. 8). The proponent of this argument simply maintains that if one is to hold to ER, then with respect to the debate as to whether to hold to ER or not, if there are good reasons to hold to ER, then those reasons must be neutral with respect to the debate between the relativist and the non-relativist.

With respect to premise 2., the relativist must claim that it is false by claiming that there can be good reasons for holding to ER *and* that those good reasons can be non-neutral (with respect to the debate between relativism and non-relativism). However, the reasons for the relativist's claim that good reasons can be non-neutral will either be neutral (which means that relativism is given up), or they will be non-neutral. However, if they are non-neutral, then why should the denial of the consequent in premise 2. be accepted over the affirmation of the consequent? Certainly the non-relativist will be free to reject that denial. Siegel argues that 'to defend relativism is to defend it non-relativistically, which is to give it up; to "defend" it relativistically is not to *defend* it at all' (p. 9).

There is some debate about whether or not the kind of criticism levelled by Siegel against ER (i.e. that relativism is incoherent because it is self-defeating) can apply to ER at all. Is there some sleight of hand going on here? Is the 'refutation' of ER the refutation of a 'straw man'? Let's consider two relativist rejoinders to the anti-relativist objection that ER is self-defeating.

One way that a philosopher might deny that ER is self-defeating is presented by Harold Zellner. Zellner has argued that like the sceptic who 'tries to convince us that the best use of reason leads to the conclusion that reason is unreliable' (Zellner 1995, p. 289), the relativist simply tries 'to show how using reason as though it were independent of culture or "conceptual frameworks," etc., leads to the opposite conclusion' (p. 289). However, Zellner's analogy of relativism with scepticism is a non-starter, because the relativist wants '*to show*' (to use Zellner's words) us something; i.e. to argue, to prove, to convince us of something. The relativist is *arguing* that argumentation (*qua* rational activity that leads to knowledge claims by means of which standards of evaluation *can* be applied) is impossible. Clearly this is self-defeating.[5]

A second rejoinder to the objection that ER is self-refuting stems from the claim that the anti-relativist plays fast and loose with the notion of truth in his criticism. For example, consider Jordan's claims that Socrates only shows that Protagoras' theory is self-defeating or incoherent because Socrates:

> equivocates between two senses of 'true,' employing 'true for . . .' when the emphasis is on what Protagoras said, and employing 'true' (irrespective of who believes what) when stating what he believes to be the fatal implication of 'man is the measure.' From 'what seems true to anyone is true for him to whom it seems so, and some men regard the foregoing proposition as false,' it follows only that that proposition is false for those to whom it seems so, not that it is false, period (Jordan 1971, p. 15).

Jordan's claim that it follows from Socrates' argument 'only that that proposition is false for those to whom it seems so' is simply false. Here is why. All that one needs to do in order to show that it is false is ask the following simple question: For *whom* is it true 'that that proposition is false for those to whom it seems so'? If the answer is 'for any subject' then relativism is given up, and Socrates' criticism is successful in showing that relativism is self-refuting, contrary to Jordan's claim. In fact, Jordan seems to indicate that this *would be* Protagoras' answer. He states, 'If I am Protagoras, I will ascribe to any proposition's denial the status of being true for those who believe it' (p. 16). This appears to be a universal claim about the nature of truth for *all* believing subjects. However, the immediate question must be put to Jordan: what is the epistemic status of *this claim itself*? If Jordan answers, it is true *simpliciter*, then relativism is given up, and the charge of self-refutation stands. However, if Jordan, or Protagoras, were to answer that this claim is true 'for me' then we no longer have an argument or an assertion of anything more than the relativist's personal belief that relativism is true. To make this move, according to Siegel, is to 'fail to join the issue with the opponent of relativism; it is to fail to assert the correctness or cognitive superiority of relativism' (Siegel 1987, p. 24).[6]

While Jordan is mistaken that Socrates' version of the self-refutation argument does not work against ER because it equivocates on 'true', Jordan ultimately argues *against* ER. He does so by recognizing that the advocate of ER is making an *assertion* about *something*, and in doing so it shows that there must be some *basis* for the relativist's claims.[7]

2nd Argument Against ER: It Leads to Solipsism (Part 1)

In addition to being self-defeating, ER leads to solipsism. Solipsism (from sola = alone and ipse = self) is a philosophical view that the only things which exist are one's self and one's thoughts. In this discussion of the general difficulties with ER, I would like to point the way towards solipsism as a potential difficulty for ER. This difficulty has been recently raised by Hilary Putnam. Putnam's criticism begins with a consideration of how solipsism might make one version of relativism consistent with the charge that it is self-refuting and concludes that solipsism, although possibly logically consistent, is no more promising as a philosophical place for relativism than its self-refuting versions.

Putnam states that there is a way to generate a consistent relativism by constructing what he calls 'first-person' relativism. 'If I am a relativist, and I define truth as to what *I* agree with, or as what I would agree with . . . then, as long as I continue to agree with my own definition of truth, the argument that my position . . . is self refuting, does not immediately arise' (Putnam 1992, p. 73). Putnam continues, 'Solipsism has never been a popular philosophical position, and first person relativism sounds dangerously close to solipsism. Indeed, it is not clear how it can avoid being solipsism' (p. 75). Relativism cannot avoid being solipsism, because

> If you and I are not the first-person relativist in question, then the truth about me and about you and about the friends and the spouse of the first-person relativist is, for the first-person relativist, simply a function of his or her own dispositions to believe. This is why first-person relativism sounds like thinly disguised solipsism. But it is hard to see why cultural relativism is any better off, in this respect. Is solipsism with a 'we' any better than solipsism with an 'I'? (p. 76).[8]

The key notion that Putnam recognizes is that the first-person relativist will maintain that truths are 'simply a function of his or her
own dispositions to believe'. Why is this similar to solipsism?
Consider the following definition of solipsism: solipsism means

> literally 'self alone', and less literally 'I alone exist' or else 'I alone
> am conscious', yielding in the first case a more idealist form of
> solipsism querying the existence of an independent material
> world, and in the second case a more materialist form allowing
> for the (possible) existence of a material world but again not
> countenancing the existence of other minds or centers of con-
> sciousness (Borst 1994, p. 487).

The solipsist will maintain that the only thing that exists is the self,
and her thoughts. The first-person relativist, according to Putnam,
is similar to the solipsist because the relativist makes what is true
dependent on the existence and aspects of the consciousness of the
relativist. The solipsist must say of herself that she alone exists and
that these things that appear to be different from herself are nothing
but her own thoughts. The first-person relativist who makes truth
dependent on her own psychological states is in the same position as
the solipsist.

The first-person relativist might say that he is not denying that
there are other minds, but that other minds do the same thing that
he does; they also make truths to be functions of *their* dispositions
to believe. However, this way out of solipsism is not open to the first-
person relativist. The first-person relativist, in making this claim, is
simply saying that this truth too is a function of his disposition to
believe it to be true.[9]

The first-person relativist has by Putnam's definition isolated
himself from other minds. This kind of isolation is seen in another
definition of solipsism, where solipsism is understood to be 'the doctrine that there exists a first person perspective possessing privileged
and irreducible characteristics, in virtue of which we stand in various
kinds of isolation from any other persons or external things that may
exist' (Vinci 1995, p. 751). The key aspect of this definition is the 'isolation' that the solipsist has from other persons.

It is in this sense of solipsism as isolation from other minds that
Burnyeat claims that if the relativist tries to escape the self-refuting
claim that 'every judgment is true *for* the person whose judgment it

is' (p. 174), by replacing it with the 'completely solipsistic claim' (p. 191), that it is only in the relativist's world that the relativist's claim is true for the relativist, then something is clearly amiss.[10] Burnyeat indicates that even the relativist's claim must:

> link judgments to something else – the world . . . though for a relativist the world has to be relativised to each individual. To speak of how things appear to someone is to describe his state of mind, but to say that things are for him as they appear is to point beyond his state of mind to the way things actually are, not indeed in the world *tout court* (for Protagoras [i.e. the relativist] there is no such thing), but in the world as it is for him, in his world (Burnyeat 1976, p. 181).

Burnyeat claims that we can make no sense of the notion that there is a world that exists only for the relativist in which his claim is true. If the relativist does not maintain that his claim is 'something we can all discuss and, possibly come to accept, but simply asserts solipsistically that he, for his part lives in a world in which this is so, then indeed there is no discussion with him' (p. 191). Thus, relativism which maintains that there is *only the relativist's world* cannot even enter into discussion about the way the world is with any other inquirer. The relativist has isolated himself from any other mind(s), and this is similar to the position of the solipsist.

Putnam's criticism against one kind of epistemological relativism, namely 'first-person relativism', seems to point the direction to a very difficult problem for relativism: it leads to solipsism. But the question at hand is whether or not Putnam's claims that first-person relativism leads to solipsism can also be applied to ER, as it is defined in this work. Does ER lead to solipsism in the same way that first-person relativism leads to solipsism? There are two difficulties that might stand in the way of an application of Putnam's argument to ER. First, Putnam's first-person relativism makes that which is true a function of what the relativist believes, and this is much different from ER, which simply maintains that knowledge claims can only be evaluated with reference to certain standards of evaluation and that given competing standards there is no way of choosing one standard over another. If it can be shown that the standards of evaluation to which ER refers are in fact the same thing as that which determines what the relativist believes, then perhaps Putnam's argument might be applied to ER.

But, this leads to a second difficulty in applying Putnam's argument to ER, namely that ER need not rely on the standards or beliefs of an individual, rather it could rely on the beliefs of a group of individuals. So, in order to make Putnam's argument count at this point, it must be shown that first-person relativism leads to ER and that a group understanding of ER is no different from the individual nature of Putnam's first-person relativism. It is clear that Putnam claims that it is hard to see why first-person solipsism is not different from 'group' solipsism, but in order to make Putnam's argument count against ER, additional arguments are needed. For the purposes of this work, Putnam's argument simply represents an additional difficulty that ER may face.

2nd Argument Against ER: It Leads to Solipsism (Part 2)

In this section, I would like to consider another argument in which Putnam claims that relativism is problematic analogously to the way in which 'methodological solipsism' is problematic. Putnam claims that a methodological solipsist is someone who maintains that

> *all* our talk can be reduced to talk about experiences and logical constructions out of experiences. More precisely he holds that everything he can conceive of is identical . . . with one or another complex of his *own* experiences. What makes him a *methodological* solipsist as opposed to a real solipsist is that he kindly adds that *you*, dear reader, are the 'I' of this construction when *you* perform it: he says *everybody* is a (methodological) solipsist (Putnam 1981, p. 236).

Putnam claims that there are two stances here which are 'ludicrously incompatible' (p. 236). On the one hand, there is the 'solipsist stance' in which the methodological solipsist claims that there is an 'asymmetry between persons': my body, your body, even your experiences are all constructed from my experiences, and 'my experiences are different from everyone else's (within the system) in that they are what *everything* is constructed from' (p. 236). But on the other hand, the methodological solipsist has another stance as well, one in which there is symmetry between persons. The solipsist says that 'you' also are the 'I' of a construction when 'you' do it, just as I am when I do it. Here Putnam points out the chief difficulty for the methodological solipsist: 'The "you" he addresses his higher-order remark to cannot be the *empirical* "you" of the system. But if it's really true that the "you" of the system is the only "you" he can *understand*, then the transcendental remark is *unintelligible*' (p. 237).

> There is an analogous problem for the cultural relativist who says, 'When I say something is *true*, I mean that it is correct according to the norms of *my* culture.' If he adds, 'When a member of a different culture says that something is true, what he means (whether he knows it or not) is that it is in conformity with the norms of *his* culture', then he is in exactly the same plight as the methodological solipsist (p. 237).

What the cultural relativist has done is simply to state that 'It is true according to the norms of *my* culture, that when a member of a different culture says something is true, what he means (whether he knows it or not) is that it is in conformity with the norms of *his* culture.' Putnam states that the cultural relativist, analogous to the methodological solipsist, makes other cultures to be 'logical constructions out of the procedures and practices' of his own culture (p. 238). The relativist's claim that 'the situation is reversed from the point of view of the *other* culture' (p. 238) will not work because the claim itself 'cannot be understood', since it is a claim of symmetry between cultural standpoints. However, such symmetry is ruled out by the relativist's own doctrine that truths are just what is correct according to the relativist's culture.

Miriam Solomon summarizes Putnam's arguments against methodological solipsism and its relativism analog in the following way:

> Just as methodological solipsism involves the claim that each person should construct the world out of his or her own experiences, relativism involves the claim that each culture sets what is rational and true, and does so independently of other cultures. Just as methodological solipsism is inconsistent because it also claims that the experiences of other people are constructions of one's own experience, relativism is inconsistent because it also claims that truth in another culture is dependent on truth in one's own culture. Neither the methodological solipsist nor the relativist can occupy a 'transcendent' point of view from which all selves, or all cultures, appear the same (Solomon 1990, p. 215).

Consider the following more formalized arguments of the argument against methodological solipsism and the analogous argument against relativism (P = person and C = culture):

The argument against methodological solipsism (MS):

1. Persons P1 and P2 construct the world from their own experiences.
2. If P1 constructs the world from her own experiences, then the experiences of P2 turn out to be constructed out of P1's experiences.
3. If the experiences of P2 turn out to be the constructions of P1's experiences, then the experiences of P2 are not the experiences of P2.
4. If the experiences of P2 are not the experiences of P2, then it is not the case that persons P1 and P2 construct the world from their own experiences.
5. Therefore, it is not the case that persons P1 and P2 construct the world out of their own experiences.

The analogous argument against relativism (RMS):

1. Propositions believed by P1 and P2 are true relative to C1 and C2 independently of other cultures.
2. If person P1 maintains that propositions are true relative to C1 independently of other cultures, then the propositions believed by P2 turn out to be true relative to C1.
3. If the propositions believed by P2 turn out to be true relative to C1, then the propositions believed by P2 are not true relative to C2 independently of other cultures.
4. If the propositions believed by P2 are not true relative to C2 independently of other cultures, then it is not the case that propositions believed by P1 and P2 are relative to C1 and C2 independently of other cultures.
5. Therefore, it is not the case that propositions believed by P1 and P2 are true relative to C1 and C2 independently of other cultures.

Miriam Solomon has raised two objections to this kind of argument presented by Putnam. First, Solomon rightly recognizes that Putnam defines truth as rational acceptability,[11] and that if one defines truth in this way and adds the relativistic claim that rational acceptability is *relative* to culture, then, barring other objections, RMS will go through. However, Solomon claims RMS will work against the relativist only if the relativist defines truth as rational acceptability relative to culture. Solomon claims, 'the relativist with respect to . . . justification, who is not also a relativist with respect to truth (and therefore does not understand truth in terms of rational acceptability) escapes Putnam's argument altogether' (Solomon 1990, p. 215). Since Putnam saddles the relativist with a definition of truth as rational acceptability relative to culture, Putnam's argument works, but if the relativist does not maintain that truth is just what is rationally acceptable in her culture, then, according to Solomon, Putnam's argument does not count against it.

Solomon is claiming that the relativist can deny premise 1., in RMS, in favour of 1′ of RMS′:

1′. Propositions believed by P1 and P2 are *justified* relative to C1 and C2 independently of other cultures.

The rest of the argument RMS′ will be the following:

2′. If person P1 maintains that propositions are *justified* relative to C1 independently of other cultures, then the propositions believed by P2 turn out to be *justified* relative to C1.

3′. If the propositions believed by P2 turn out to be *justified* relative to C1, then the propositions believed by P2 are not *justified* relative to C2 independently of other cultures.

4′. If the propositions believed by P2 are not *justified* relative to C2 independently of other cultures, then it is not the case that propositions believed by P1 and P2 are relative to C1 and C2 independently of other cultures.

5′. Therefore, it is not the case that propositions believed by P1 and P2 are *justified* relative to C1 and C2 independently of other cultures.

Solomon thinks that the relativist who maintains 1′ will not be subject to the difficulties of RMS. However, this kind of relativist, a relativist about justification, will fall prey to the argument as well. It will turn out that all propositions justified by P2 are justified by C1 and not by C2 independently of other cultures and this results in the same kind of contradiction as the relativist about truth. The form of the argument counts against both relativism about truth and relativism about justification. Solomon is wrong in thinking that the conclusion of RMS can be avoided by maintaining relativism with respect to justification. The reason that RMS works is not because of relativism about truth; it is because of *relativism*.

Solomon's key claim in her first objection to RMS is that one can be a relativist about truth but not about justification. However, it is unclear that an understanding of relativism about justification is even an understanding of justification. The usual understanding of justification (whether it be foundationalist, or coherentist) is that justification is that which provides some reason or indication that a belief is true. To claim that justification can be relative and truth not relative is to talk about something other than justification, since justification carries with it an element of truth indicativeness.[12] So, it is unclear whether Solomon's claim that one can be a relativist about justification and not be a relativist about truth is in fact, as she puts it, 'a genuine epistemological position' (p. 220, footnote 3).

The second objection that Solomon raises against RMS is that RMS is not analogous with MS. That is, the positions of the methodological solipsist and the relativist are not analogous. The central focus here seems to be the analogy between premise 2 of MS and premise 2 of RMS. Solomon is willing to allow that premise 2 of MS is true, but that premise 2 of RMS is not, and it is here that Solomon claims that the analogy breaks down. Solomon claims that it is not inconsistent to maintain both that the propositions believed by P2 (and that are relative to C2) turn out to be true relative to C1, and that C2 functions as that which determines the truth of propositions for P2 independently of other cultures, including C1. According to Solomon, C2 is causally independent from C1 in making beliefs true for P2. Solomon adds that P1 need not claim that P2 has C1 or that P1 chooses C2 for P2. Thus, unlike premise 2 of MS in which P1 constructs reality for P2, in premise 2 of RMS, P1 does not construct C2 for P2.

Consider this rather lengthy quotation from Solomon, which shows how C1 might be causally independent from C2. Solomon uses the example of President Bush making a choice between two decisions to make her point. Solomon states:

> Suppose Bush makes a choice between two alternatives: 'Pursue the Tower nomination' and 'Abandon the Tower nomination.' According to RR [P1], Bush's choice is, as every fact, culturally determined. Yet RR [P1] can still give an account of Bush's

autonomy in the usual way, in terms of psychological and environmental causes of Bush's decision. To be sure, these causes – as all states of the world – are culturally determined also. But there is no inconsistency in saying *both* that Bush's decision was culturally determined and that it was a *decision,* i.e., arrived at by some chain of causes having to do with Bush's psychological states and environmental factors and causally independent of the social facts determining truths. Similarly, there is no obvious inconsistency in saying *both* that Karl's [P2's] truths are determined by the norms of RR's [P1's] society [C1] and that Karl's [P2's] norms are *norms,* i.e., rules of Karl's [P2's] society which are socially inculcated and have various histories, often causally independent of RR's [P1's] society [C1]. Autonomy, in the sense required for describing both Bush's decision and German norms [C2], requires only this causal independence. RR [P1] is *not* saying either that Karl [P2] has our [P1's] norms, or that we [P1] choose Karl's [P2's] norms (p. 217).

Thus, according to Solomon, Putnam has failed to show that MS and RMS are analogous.

While Putnam does not respond directly to Solomon's argument, given what he does say, he might respond by saying that Solomon is simply wrong in thinking that C2 can be causally independent from C1 in making beliefs true for P2. Putnam explicitly states that a culture like C2 will 'become, so to speak, logical constructions out of the procedures and practices' (Putnam 1981, p. 238) of C1. Putnam's claim is correct. According to Putnam, when P1 asserts premise 1. of RMS above, P1 is making a claim about C2. However, P1's claim about P2's C2 can only be true in P1's C1, just as P2 is nothing but something constructed out of P1's experiences in MS. Putnam makes it clear that when P1 utters premise 1. of RMS, P2's C2 becomes internally linked to P1's C1, and cannot be independent in any sense. Thus, Putnam's saying that P2's C2 is what makes something true for P2 cannot be understood as anything other than a mere reflection of P1's C1.[13] Thus, the cases are parallel, and Solomon's objection has missed Putnam's main point in the analogy.

In attempting to argue against Putnam's objection to relativism based on an analogy to solipsism, Solomon is defending relativism. She claims that there is a way to make relativism free from charges of incoherence. She states,

I contend, however, that the relativist is free to state her position so that it is a doctrine about the concept of truth in the culture from which the doctrine is propounded, not a doctrine about the concept of truth in all cultures. Thus stated, the doctrine is not vulnerable to being falsified by finding that another culture denies the truth of relativism [the argument derived from Plato] (p. 218).[14]

This formulation of relativism is not very philosophically interesting, and is certainly not what most people who claim to be relativists actually claim. The relativist normally claims something like premise 1. in RMS. The relativist doesn't make a claim for herself alone, but she claims that for every person, truth will be relative to their culture. Let us put Solomon's claim here in Putnam's terminology: what the relativist is saying is 'When I say something is *true*, I mean that it is correct according to the norms of *my* culture' (Putnam 1981, p. 237). This might simply be a descriptive account of what the members of a culture think truth is, but it can carry no weight other than that.

CONCLUSION

Epistemological relativism may have an important philosophical lesson to teach us, mostly with respect to the first part of its definition (i.e. the 'standards conjunction'). The idea that every truth claim, every item of knowledge has some standard by means of which it is evaluated or understood to be a truth claim, as opposed to merely a belief, seems important for a general theory of what it is to come to know something. This point while not unique to relativism about knowledge is one that is important in general for doing epistemology. The second part of the definition of epistemic relativism, however, is what contributes to the self-defeating or solipsistic consequences of taking the view seriously in one's account of knowledge. Thus, it should be rejected.

CHAPTER 3

ONTOLOGICAL RELATIVISM

INTRODUCTION

Whereas epistemological relativism may seem close to home, or something that one might hear on talk radio or on the evening news (e.g. 'That's true for you . . .'), ontological relativism is a type of relativism that may seem far removed from one's normal everyday experiences. Ontological or metaphysical relativism is a version of relativism where the very nature of reality or specific things that are real are thought to derive their existence or their natures from some activity of the human mind or beliefs or practices from within a particular culture. One way of illustrating this type of relativism about what is real can be shown by an examination of various drawings or sketches which are, as John Kihlstrom has pointed out, 'ambiguous (or reversible or bistable)' (Kihlstrom 2004). One example is of a picture, the famous 'duck-rabbit'. This first sketch of the duck-rabbit was originally published by Joseph Jastrow (see Kihlstrom 2004), and is similar to a simplified version presented by Ludwig Wittgenstein in his *Philosophical Investigations* (Wittgenstein 1953). An additional type of Gestalt drawing was referred to by Edwin G. Boring (Boring 1930, p. 444), an American psychologist early in the 20th century. It is ambiguous between a young and an old woman.

The idea that is often inferred from such ambiguous drawings is that human cognition functions as a constructive tool to create a visual reality of our own making. The inference then is something like this: if it is possible to do such constructing in simple cases, perhaps much of what we think is objective reality is nothing more than the mind's construction. Thus, what is real, what exists (either in part or whole), is relative to human interests. In what follows, we will briefly consider a general statement of ontological relativism followed by a general argument against it. Then, we will take a little case study of one attempt to present a version of ontological relativism that avoids the pitfalls of the general arguments against it. This case study will examine Hilary Putnam's 'conceptual relativity'. I will argue that Putnam's conceptual relativism has inherent problems similar to the problems of a generalized ontological relativism.

GENERAL FORMULATION AND PROBLEMS WITH ONTOLOGICAL RELATIVISM

An ontological relativist would try to argue that what is real is determined (in part or whole) by the human mind. There are at least two types of argument against any philosophical view that maintains the strong ontological claim that language, concepts, thought, etc., literally make the world we live in.[1]

First, consider the following: language (thoughts, concepts, beliefs) being what it is cannot create reality being what it is (e.g. desks, chairs, cars, numbers, etc.). This might be rejected for cases of human action, e.g. my belief that my flight leaves at 5:00pm creates the reality of my arriving at the airport, through my action of driving there, or my linguistic statement to my introduction to philosophy class, 'There's a quiz on Descartes' *Meditations* today' creates a kind of (usually quite uncomfortable) social reality.[2] However, the human mind (the realm of beliefs, concepts, language) has properties that do not by themselves have what it takes to generate real things that are independent of the mind. Just try it. Try, just by believing that there is petrol in your tank sufficient to power your car to your destination. Belief alone is insufficient.

Second, consider the following: if language (concepts, beliefs, thoughts) constructs reality, it will be because of what language (concepts, beliefs, thoughts) *really is*. Thus, not all of reality can be constructed by language (concepts, beliefs, thoughts). These things that do the construction turn out to be themselves *un-constructed*. Thus, not all of reality is constructed.

One of the motivations for ontological relativism flows from the philosophy of Immanuel Kant.[3] Kant was certainly not a relativist; the categories of the understanding were the same for all human beings, providing a kind of neutral standard for judgement. However, Kant's contribution to features of ontological relativism can be seen in his notion that the categories of the understanding structure the phenomena of our experiences coming to us from the noumenal (unconditioned and unknown world). If one drops the Kantian notion of categories of the understanding shared by all human knowers and replaces it with the notion that each of us has our own (or culturally generated) constructivist lenses such that there is no neutrality between them, then relativism follows. Yet, these lenses themselves appear to be immune from construction; thus not all of reality is constructed.

A CASE STUDY OF ONTOLOGICAL RELATIVISM: HILARY PUTNAM'S CONCEPTUAL RELATIVISM

In *The Many Faces of Realism*, Hilary Putnam tries to

> show that rejecting the project of Ontology – of a description of things as they are 'apart from our conceptual systems' – does not put an end to all the interesting questions about language and thought; rather it calls attention to phenomenon we have been downplaying (when we do not actually ignore them), for example, the phenomenon which I called conceptual relativity (Putnam 1987, p. 86).

In what follows, we will first examine Putnam's rejection of the project of Ontology. Second, we will examine his positive arguments for conceptual relativity. Third, we will show why that position is problematic.

What is Putnam's rejection of the project of Ontology? Putnam partly answers this question in his historical discussion of the metaphysical views of Locke and Descartes in which there is supposed to be a sharp distinction between primary and secondary qualities. It is not clear whether or not Putnam agrees with Locke and Descartes or merely describes their views. It seems to me that Putnam will agree with the following claim, although for different reasons than do Descartes and Locke. The claim is, 'the idea that there is a property all red objects have in common – the same in all cases – and another property all green objects have in common – the same in all cases – is a kind of illusion, on the view we have come more and more to take for granted since the age of Descartes and Locke' (p. 6). The reason that I think Putnam ultimately agrees with this view can be seen in a consideration of the following statement: 'The deep systematic root of the disease, I want to suggest, lies in the notion of an "intrinsic" property, a property something has "in itself", apart from any contribution made by language or the mind' (p. 8). Putnam maintains that some properties are intrinsic and others extrinsic, or projections that we give to objects. This division corresponds to the primary (intrinsic) and secondary (extrinsic) properties of Descartes and Locke who maintain that there are two very different kinds of properties. There are properties that really are 'out there in the objects', and others that aren't really 'out there', but are just 'in our minds' (or 'in our heads').

It seems to me that there are at least six alternatives to this bifurcation of properties.

1. One can simply bite the bullet and cling to this sort of property dualism (I use the term dualism in a special sense here: a duality of properties . . . some in our heads and some in the world), but this view seems to degenerate into either the second, third, fourth or fifth option.
2. One can take the primary qualities and stick them in the mind; this is Berkeleyen idealism.
3. One can take the primary qualities and stick them in the head (literally in the brain, or in the brain's behaviours) and you have reductive materialism.
4. One can take the primary and secondary qualities and stick them in our language usage, and this yields a form of ontological relativism.
5. One can take the primary and secondary qualities and make them 'plastic' enough to be sort of out there in the objects, but dependent for their being what they are on our interests; this is Putnam's conceptual ontological relativism.
6. One can take the primary and secondary qualities and stick them both back out there in the objects; this is what Putnam understands to be Plato's, Aristotle's and Aquinas' option.

Putnam's rejection of the project of Ontology amounts to this: a rejection of the first, second, third, fourth and sixth options. We will not examine Putnam's rejection of options 1–3, and option 4 Putnam rejects on the ground that relativism in general is both self-defeating and leads to solipsism. What exactly does Putnam mean by conceptual relativity? Conceptual relativity (also called internal realism and pragmatic realism and most recently 'pluralistic realism'[4]) is Putnam's way of avoiding the modern philosophers' bifurcation of properties (option 1, in the list above). Putnam claims that pluralistic realism preserves 'common sense realism while avoiding the absurdities and antinomies' of the options listed above. Why does he tack on the 'realism' part to the relativism part? Putnam insists that 'realism is not incompatible with conceptual relativity. One can be both a realist and a conceptual relativist' (p. 17). He explains that by realism he means 'taking our commonsense schemes at face value . . . without helping [ourselves] to the notion of the thing "in itself" ' (p. 17).

By conceptual relativity Putnam does not mean 'there is no truth to be found'. What he does mean, he tries to show by example.[5] Putnam asks us to consider a world with three individuals, x1, x2, x3, and ask, 'How many objects are there in this world?' (p. 18). Putnam claims that the answer to this question is relative to the concepts that we use to take account of the objects. One possible way to answer this question is to say that there are simply three objects: x1, x2 and x3. A second possible way to answer the question is to say, with the Polish logicians like Lezniewski, that 'for every two particulars there is an object which is their sum' (p. 18). Thus, this answer would be there are seven objects: x1, x2, x3, x1+x2, x1+x3, x2+x3, x1+x2+x3. Putnam claims that the phenomenon of conceptual relativity 'turns on the fact that the logical primitives themselves, and in particular the notions of object and existence, have a multitude of different uses rather than one absolute meaning' (p. 19). Again he says, 'the idea that there is an Archimedean point, or a use of "exist" inherent in the world itself, from which the question "How many objects really exist?" makes sense, is an illusion' (p. 20). Putnam summarizes his task in presenting this example at the end of his second lecture in *The Many Faces of Realism*. He states,

> Given a language, we can describe the 'facts' that make the sentences of that language true and false in a 'trivial' way – using the sentences of that very language; but the dream of finding a well-defined Universal Relation between a (supposed) totality of all facts and an arbitrary true sentence in an arbitrary language, is just the dream of an absolute notion of a fact (or of an 'object') and of an absolute relation between sentences and the facts (or the objects) 'in themselves'; the very dream whose hopelessness

I hoped to expose with the aid of my little example involving three
Carnapian individuals and seven non-empty mereological sums
(p. 40).

Putnam's view is clearly expressed when he states, 'What we cannot
say – because it makes no sense – is what the facts are independent
of all conceptual choices'.

One motivation for Putnam's ontological relativism comes from
the American pragmatist philosopher William James. Putnam presents James' view as it is given in a letter to one of James' critics,
Dickinson S. Miller. James states,

> The world per se may be likened to a cast of beans on a table. By
> themselves they spell nothing. An onlooker may group them as
> he likes. He may simply count them all and map them. He may
> select groups and name these capriciously, or name them to suit
> certain extrinsic purposes of his. Whatever he does, so long as he
> takes account of them, his account is neither false nor irrelevant.
> If neither, why not call it true? It fits the beans-minus-him, and
> expresses the total fact of beans-plus-him. Truth in this total
> sense is partially ambiguous, then. If he simply counts or maps,
> he obeys a subjective interest as much as if he traces figures. Let
> that stand for pure 'intellectual' treatment of the beans, while
> grouping them variously stands for non-intellectual interest. All
> that . . . I contend for is that there is no 'truth' without some inter-
> est, and that non-intellectual interests play a part as well as the
> intellectual ones. Whereupon we are accused of denying the
> beans, or denying being in any way constrained by them! It's too
> silly! (James 1926, p. 295).

Putnam discusses this letter at length and states that according to
James, 'the public world we experience is not a "ready-made"
world . . . no single unique description is imposed upon us by non-
human reality' (p 14). Putnam elaborates in detail on this discussion
in his Dewey Lectures. After summarizing James' view, Putnam considers the view of what he calls a 'traditional realist philosopher'
(Putnam 1994, p. 448), who might respond to James by saying,

> The reason such a classification is possible, and can be extended
> to other similar collections of beans in the future, is that there

are such properties as colors, sizes, adjacency, etc. Your beloved 'interests' may determine which combinations of properties you regard as worth talking about or even lead you to invent a name for things with a particular combination of properties if there is no such name already in the language, but it does not change the world in the slightest. The world is as it is independently of the interests of any describer (p. 448).

Putnam makes it clear that he agrees with the traditional metaphysical claims that 'when I talk about anything that is not causally effected by my own interests . . . I can also say that the world would be the same in that respect even if I did not have those interests, had not given that description, etc. And with all that I agree' (footnote 7, p. 448). In addition, Putnam rejects what he considers James' view that 'the world we know is to an indeterminate extent the product of our own mind'.

The key point in understanding Putnam's ontological relativism can be found by examining the rejection of the traditional metaphysical realist's criticisms of James' account as metaphysical fantasy. The fantasy in question is the traditional realist's view that 'there is a totality of "forms" or "universals" or "properties" fixed once and for all, and that every possible meaning of a word corresponds to one of these "forms" or "universals" or "properties." The structure of all possible thoughts is fixed in advance – fixed by the "forms" ' (p. 448).[6]

Putnam expresses this in a slightly different way at the beginning of his second Dewey Lectures. He criticizes the traditional view of metaphysical realism with its 'idea that there is a definite totality of all objects, and a definite totality of all "properties" ' (p. 466). These are also views about knowledge claims which are

about the distribution of 'properties' over the 'objects,'. . . there is a definite totality of all possible knowledge claims, likewise fixed once and for all independently of language users or thinkers. The nature of the language users or the thinkers can determine which of the possible knowledge claims they are able to think or verbalize, but not what the possible knowledge claims are (p. 466).

Putnam indicates that these forms of metaphysical realism (I'm not sure if he counts these as the traditional forms or just naturalistic forms of realism) go hand in hand with causal theories of perception. He recognizes that previous metaphysical realism prior to the 17th century was predominantly Aristotelian. Putnam quotes Aristotle, 'the thinking part of the soul, while impassible, must be capable of receiving the form of an object; that is must be potentially the same as its object without being the object' (Aristotle 1995, *De Anima* Book 429 a14–7). Although Putnam rejects causal theories of perception in favour of something else, he does not accept Aristotle's view *tout court*. He states,

> We are puzzled by Aristotle's theory because we do not under-stand in what sense the mind 'becomes' hot or cold (even 'poten-tially' if not actually hot or cold) when it perceives something hot or cold, or in what sense the mind becomes 'potentialy' spherical when it perceives a bronze sphere, or becomes 'potentially' a par-ticular rational animal when it perceives a man (p. 467).

However, he appears to be willing to accept Aristotle's view that we really do perceive properties in objects and not 'events inside our-selves . . . caused by them' (p. 467).

Here is the key to understanding Putnam's project: 'we need to revive the spirit of the older view, though without the metaphysical baggage (for example, the mind "becoming" its objects, though only "potentially," or the mind taking on the "form" of the object per-ceived "without its matter")' (p. 469). Putnam indicates that William James was the first modern philosopher to present such a view.

What exactly is Putnam's problem with the traditional realist's view as he construes it? Putnam claims that there are two problems with the older Aristotelian view. The first problem is the metaphysi-cal realist's putative *naïveté* about meaning. This *naïveté* consists in the belief that 'the meaning of a word is a property shared by all the things denoted by the word' (p. 449). That this is naïve, Putnam claims, is because there are obvious counter examples in which the ordinary meaning of words like 'gold' 'cannot be expressed as a property or a conjunction of properties at all' (p. 449).

The second problem for the metaphysical realist is the twofold assumption that '[a.] there is one definite totality of objects that can be classified and [b.] one definite totality of all "properties"' (p. 449). Putnam agrees, as was indicated above, that there is something true in these assumptions, namely that 'a knowledge claim is responsible to reality . . . independent of the speaker' (p. 449). However, there is something that is clearly false, according to Putnam, about these two assumptions. Again, as in the first problem, he provides counter examples (three different kinds in this case) that are supposed to show 'that neither the form of all knowledge claims nor the ways in which they are responsible to reality is fixed once and for all in advance' (p. 449).

First, he indicates that realities such as wars or events in general, the sky, mirror images, and objects of desire or intentional objects (one's thought of Santa Claus) don't seem to be 'objects' at all. Second, Putnam considers the difficulty of mereological sums that also don't seem to be objects that are fixed. He states, 'One ancient criterion for being a single object is that the parts of a single object move with the object when the object is moved'. The difficulty here is the parts of objects, like a lamp that has its shade fall off when it is moved. Putnam asks 'Is the lamp then not an object?' (p. 450). Third, he presents views about quantum mechanics which show that 'with the development of knowledge our idea of what counts as even a possible knowledge claim, our idea of what counts as even a possible object, and our idea of what counts as even a possible property are all subject to change' (p. 451).

After presenting these counter examples, Putnam reminds his reader that he agrees with the traditional realist that there is an independent reality and that we have a 'cognitive responsibility to do justice to whatever we describe' (p. 452). However, he is quick also to distance himself from the traditional metaphysician by claiming to recognize a 'real insight in James's pragmatism, the insight that "description" is never a mere copying and that we constantly add to the ways in which language can be responsible to reality' (p. 452). And it is this that makes Putnam's views ontologically relativistic. Reality is conditioned in some way by human interests, specifically human language.

DIFFICULTIES WITH PUTNAM'S ONTOLOGICAL RELATIVISM

What kinds of criticism can be aimed at Putnam's rejection of the traditional realist perspective that yields his relativism? There are at least two lines of criticism that can be pursued. First, I would like to take up the analysis of the spilled beans from a traditional metaphysical realist perspective in the way that Putnam has painted this view. I would like to show the absurdities of Putnam's views with regard to the beans. Second, I would like to offer a traditional metaphysical realist rejoinder to Putnam's objections.

Suppose I spill a can of beans on my kitchen table. I immediately, in James' words, 'take account of them'. It seems to me that the first way that I take account of them is by recognizing that these are beans and not bananas or mice that have spilled out of the can. James, and Putnam with him, claim 'there is no "truth" without some interest' (James), and ' "description" is never a mere copying' (Putnam). There are two questions, the answers to which seem to be either true or false, that must be asked at this point regarding the ontology of that which is spilled on my kitchen table. The first question is 'Do these things exist independently of me?' Putnam makes it clear that he is not denying the beans' existence. The second question is 'Are these things the kinds of things they are independently of me?' I think Putnam would have to reply 'No'. He would have to reply this way because of his statement that there are no truths apart from some interest. If there were no interest, there would be no truth to the question 'Are these things on my table beans?', if I have no interest in them. There is nothing in the beans themselves, no property or group of properties that makes them essentially beans and not some other thing.

Remember, Putnam stated, 'the public world we experience is not a "ready-made" world'. Thus, the beans we experience are not 'ready-made' beans. We somehow help make them. Putnam denies that there is a 'single unique description [that] is imposed upon us by non-human reality' (p. 14). Thus, there is no unique description imposed on us by the beans *qua* beans. What could this possibly mean with respect to the questions posed above? It means the following: there is no single unique description of whether or not the beans exist independently of me, and there is no single description of whether or not the beans are what they are independently of me.

In Putnam's words, if I pick one of the things that I have spilled on my table, and I describe this thing as something that exists independently of me and is a bean independently of my interests, what I certainly have not done is given a 'description' that somehow copies these properties from the reality which I am describing. What I have done, or so Putnam would have us believe, is somehow added my interests to the 'reality' in question.

However, Putnam admits that in some ways the beans are what they are regardless of our interests. Yet, he denies that the beans are what they are in virtue of their having some essential or intrinsic property that makes them beans. We might ask what makes them beans, and what makes them exist as beans? Even if Putnam can put forth an adequate answer to this question, Putnam's claims are still in trouble. Putnam's claim that there is 'no unique description that is imposed upon us by non-human reality' is self-defeating. The claim itself is apparently a description of non-human reality that seems to be a claim of what that reality is uniquely like. But this is what Putnam is denying.

Even so, Putnam proceeds to criticize the traditional metaphysician. Let me restate his presentation above of the view of the metaphysical realist in terms of the spilled beans. My interests may determine how I 'take account' of the beans, but they don't change the beans *qua* beans in the slightest. The beans are as they are independently of the interests of any describer. What is a metaphysical fantasy, according to Putnam, in the beans example is that the beans have forms or properties or universals to which words about them must correspond in order for us to describe the beans correctly or truly. In other words, the metaphysical realist is saying that the 'structure of all possible thoughts [about the beans *qua* beans] is fixed in advance – fixed by the forms' (p. 448). Is this true for the questions asked above? Is the existence of these things constrained by the forms which according to Aristotle make a thing exist, and exist as the kinds (in this case bean-kind) of things they are? Let us assume that Putnam's answer is no. Then, what is the basis for these things existing, and existing as the kinds of things they are?

Let me give a traditional metaphysical realist rejoinder to Putnam's objections. Let us take the word 'bean'. I suppose Putnam would say that the meaning of this word can't be 'expressed as a property or a conjunction of properties at all' (p. 449), which allows me to refer correctly to these things spilled on my kitchen table as beans. Well, what is the meaning of the word 'bean'? The metaphysical realist could say something like the following: the word 'bean' is determined by a fixed group of properties in my mind, and whenever that group of fixed properties matches up with the properties of the object that I perceive, I describe correctly that which I have in front of me as a bean.

Perhaps this discussion has to be carried out at the deeper level of what meaning amounts to. The metaphysical realist would not need to express any *naïveté* about meaning and think that 'the meaning of a word is a property shared by all the things denoted by the word' (p. 449). The metaphysical realist could construe meaning in terms of a range of properties that are contained in a concept, and a word's meaning is constrained by the range of properties contained in that concept. When has a word been used correctly? (The word 'concept' can be translated literally as 'grab-with'.) A word is used correctly just in case one grabs the thing which the grab-with is of. How is this done? It is done with an account of an awareness of the matching of universals in a perceptual experience. When you see the match of the universals in the percept and in the concept in a perceptual experience the concept is fulfilled by the percept. The 'grab-with' grabs on to reality. The word is used correctly in just these cases. So the person using the word bean has to specify what they mean by the word bean. They do this by describing the properties they have in mind when they use the word. A metaphysical realist of the traditional variety could say that words can mean whatever you want them to mean, but concepts cannot. This route might circumvent Putnam's first problem with the traditional metaphysicalist view.

The second metaphysical view according to Putnam, again as stated in terms of the beans, is that there is 'one definite totality' of beans 'that can be classified and one definite totality of all "properties"' of the beans. Yes, the traditional metaphysical realist would say that the spilled beans do constitute a definite totality with respect to their existing and their existing as beans, and there is a definite totality of properties had by the beans as beans.

Let us consider one bean. What would it mean to say that this bean does not have one definite totality with respect to its existence and to its being what it is? And, what would it mean to say that this bean does not have one definite totality of properties? I suppose we could divide the answer to these questions into ontological versions and epistemological versions. It may very well be the case that we can never give an exhaustive description of the definite totality of properties had by the bean, or give a complete list of the properties of the bean. However, it does not follow that there is no definite totality to the existence or totality of properties of the nature of the bean.

There are two ways around Putnam's claim that traditional metaphysical realists talk of reality as a totality of fixed and determinate 'objects'. First, the traditional metaphysical realist could simply try to specify what is meant by 'objects', and show that in every case that

Putnam presents, these things do count as objects. This seems like a long and arduous task for the traditional metaphysical realist. Perhaps an easier path for the traditional metaphysical realist is to do away with talk about fixed objects. Talk about 'objects' could be replaced with talk about instantiated universals. The traditional metaphysical realist could talk about the totality of instantiated universals, and claim that many of these instantiated universals are instanced as determinate objects, and others are not. There would still be a fixed totality to which our thoughts or propositions could correspond, but this fixed totality in some ways does fall into definite objects, and in others not. The metaphysical realist might claim with respect to the beans spilled on the table that the beans on the table have certain properties that make these things beans, instead of bananas or mice. These properties are intrinsic to the beans themselves and are what allow us to recognize that they exist and that they exist as beans.

Even if this route fails, Putnam's claim is still in trouble. He claims that it is a metaphysical fantasy that there is a totality of forms. What is Putnam doing in this criticism? He seems to be saying that reality is a certain kind of way. Yet, is this description itself fixed once and for all? Is this the way the ontological universe is? If so, then Putnam's claim is self-defeating. If it is not, then why does he make the claim at all? This seems to be a bit of relativism that Putnam is saddled with in spite of his claims to avoid this sort of thing. Perhaps any account that contains in it the key aspects of relativism in any form doesn't amount to a hill of beans.

CONCLUSION

The type of ontological relativism we have been dealing with in this chapter is one of several types of ontological relativism (e.g. Quine 1969).[7] I have argued that any version of ontological relativism which claims that it is about reality contains in it a logical problem of self-referential incoherence. In any ontological relativism in which reality is relative to something else, that something else will be real or it will not be real. If it is real then ontological relativism is given up. If it is not real, then nothing can *be* relative to it and thus ontological relativism is given up. Further, if any account of ontological relativism is about what is real, then ontological relativism must be given up as well.

CHAPTER 4

ETHICAL RELATIVISM

INTRODUCTION

'Who are you to judge?' 'That might be right for you, but it's not right for me!' These are some common, everyday locutions of ethical relativism that one might often hear around the dinner table at a family gathering or in the break room when a hot topic in the realm of ethics comes up, whether it be the morality of warfare or abortion or euthanasia or whatever. Ethical relativism is a species of relativism in general:

Relativism = df:

> The nature and existence of items of knowledge, qualities, values or logical entities non-trivially obtain their natures and/or existence from certain aspects of human activity, including, but not limited to, beliefs, cultures, languages, etc.

In the case of ethical relativism, the relativistic position is one in which the reality of moral values themselves obtains their goodness or 'oughtness' from either an individual's own moral preferences, or through the beliefs and practices of the culture in which one finds oneself. Ethical relativism is probably the most common form of relativism in our culture. We live in an ethically pluralistic age. With the rise of instantaneous global communication, the blending of cultures into cosmopolitan 'tossed salads', we are confronted on a daily basis with a wide array of appeals to radical differences in views on how we should live our lives ethically. For example, the death penalty is accepted in some parts of the world and is condemned in other parts of the world. Such situations often lead people to believe that ethics are simply relative to individual or personal preference. Proponents of ethical relativism often offer two justifications in its favour: 1. The argument from cultural variance; 2. The argument from tolerance. Let us treat each of these in turn.

THE ARGUMENT FROM CULTURAL VARIANCE

One of the most famous anthologized passages in introductory readers' ethics on moral relativism comes from the early 20th century in the discipline of anthropology from a book entitled *Patterns in Culture* by Ruth Benedict (Benedict 1934).[1] In this text, Benedict cites several examples of how what is thought to be normal in one culture is often thought to be abnormal in another. This does not necessarily apply only to trivial things, e.g. it's normal to drive on the right side of the road in the US, but not normal to do so in the UK. This case of differences of driving merely instances one moral (or at least social) belief differently applied: i.e. find a consistent, safe way to conduct your society's driving habits and apply them accordingly. Whether one picks the right or the left side of the road, as long as the rules are applied consistently, the general moral principle that one ought to drive safely can be maintained, regardless of how that principle is applied.

Benedict's claim is a bit stronger than this. The claim she appears to be making is that cultures differ radically in their beliefs about what in fact are the basic norms of the day. One example is of the Kwakiutl people indigenous to the northwest coast of Canada. The example Benedict offers is one in which the tribe suffers the death of one of its members through an accident or some other non-war related incident. This death is a great affront to the dignity of the tribe, and in order to make things right from this offence to their dignity, the tribe would mount a war party and set off to take the life of a tribe member of a neighbouring tribe. In that culture, affront killings were a normal course of what ought to be done. There would be no legal or social retributions put upon the members of the tribe who killed members of the neighbouring tribe. Suppose however that the killing took place in the Bay Area of California, where one resident of San Francisco were killed in a bicycle accident, and in order to make up for this offensive loss, the woman's family drove across the San Francisco Bay to Oakland, and shot and killed the first residents of Oakland that they came across. This would not be thought to be a normal action in San Francisco. In fact, if these individuals were caught by the police, they would most likely, if convicted, go to prison for a very long time. So in the culture of the Kwakiutl, it is normal to execute neighbouring tribesmen to make up for the loss of a loved one, but in the culture of San Francisco it is not.

So far all we have is a form of *descriptive* ethical relativism. Descriptive ethical relativism is roughly the empirical claim that cultures do in fact differ in their ethical beliefs and practices. The hard work of sociologists, anthropologists, ethnologists among others has contributed greatly to our understanding of the myriad ways in which cultures differ in their ethical beliefs. It seems possible to relate this notion of descriptive ethical relativism to the definition of epistemic relativism given above, but modified slightly to show how one moves from descriptive ethical relativism to prescriptive ethical relativism. Consider again the 'standards' conjunct in Siegel's definition of epistemic relativism:

> For any knowledge-claim [including claims about ethics] p, p can be evaluated (assessed, established, etc.) only according to (with reference to) one or another set of background principles and standards of evaluation $s_1, \ldots s_n$.

So far, Benedict's claim applies only to the standards conjunct in this definition of relativism. The Kwakiutl's belief p: 'killing a neighbouring tribesman to make up for our loss is moral' was established by them with reference to a background principle or standard of evaluation s: the common practices of the tribe. The work of the sociologist and anthropologist is to clarify what exactly those practices are and what exactly are the standards of justification offered from within the tribe. This is empirical work, and often quite difficult to do in light of linguistic translation and the novelty of experience with ideas that are new and different. But the standards conjunct in the definition of relativism is not the whole picture of epistemological relativism applied to the area of ethics. We might say at this point that descriptive ethical relativism is nothing more than an acceptance of the standards conjunct in the definition of philosophical relativism offered by Siegel.

There is nothing at all philosophically problematic about an acceptance of the empirical claims made by a descriptive ethical relativist. It is simply a fact that cultures differ in their moral beliefs and practices. What is problematic, both logically and practically, is the move from descriptive ethical relativism to *prescriptive* ethical relativism. Prescriptive ethical relativism is roughly the view that not only do cultures differ in their moral beliefs, but there is no right or wrong way to say which culture is better in its particular beliefs and practices. This is tantamount to an acceptance of the 'no neutrality' conjunct of the definition of relativism that we are operating with here:

> and, given a different set (or sets) of background principles and standards s_1', . . . s_n', there is no neutral (that is, neutral with respect to the two (or more) alternative sets of principles and standards) way of choosing between the two (or more) alternative sets in evaluating p with respect to truth or rational justification. p's truth and rational justifiability are relative to the standards used in evaluating p (Siegel 1987, p. 6).

In the case at hand, the *prescriptive* relativist would agree with the *descriptive* relativist that cultures do in fact differ in their ethical beliefs, but would add the normative (i.e. prescriptive) element to the descriptive claim that there is no neutral way to determine who is right in their ethical beliefs, the Kwakiutl tribesmen or the citizens of contemporary San Francisco, for example. The former base their belief that it is moral to kill their neighbours to make up for their own loss on their internal tribal standards, and contemporary San Franciscans base their belief that killing neighbouring citizens of Oakland is immoral on the constitutional values of US laws that protect the innocent. The descriptive relativist (and this is just what ethicists usually mean when they speak of ethical relativists) would claim that there is no neutral way to choose who is right in this case, since each group of people has differing standards of how to evaluate their respective actions. Given one set of standards, the act is right/moral/good, and given another set of standards, the act is wrong/immoral/bad. Who are we to judge, given the fact that there are no neutral standards of ethical evaluation?

Benedict appears to be making such a move as she identifies from her particular cases that what is thought to be normal in a culture is simply determined by the practices of a culture. She states,

We do not make the mistake of deriving the morality of our locality and decade directly from the inevitable constitution of human nature. We do not elevate it to the dignity of a first principle. We recognize that morality differs in every society, and is a convenient term for socially approved habits (p. 536).

She then adds, 'Historically, the two phrases [it is morally good and it is habitual] are synonymous.' This appears, however, to be a denial of neutrality, or as she puts it a 'first principle'.

A formalization of this type of argument might look like this:

1. Cultures radically differ in their moral beliefs, especially in the justification that they give for those beliefs.
2. If cultures radically differ in their moral beliefs, then there are no neutral standards by means of which to evaluate those beliefs.
3. If there are no neutral standards by means of which to evaluate a culture's ethical beliefs, then ethics itself (i.e. what is morally right or wrong) is simply relative to the standards of evaluation had within a culture.
4. Therefore, given 1–3, ethics are culturally relative.

There are several problems with this argument. First, it is self-defeating. Second, it is based on an unreasonable connection between differences in beliefs and a rejection of the possibility of objective morality. Third, premise 1 is false; cultures may differ in some cases in the application of moral truths, but not always radically about basic moral truths. Let us examine these objections in turn.

Ethical Relativism is Self-Defeating

In the argument above for ethical relativism, premises are offered as being reasonably thought to be true, and a conclusion is given that is reasonably thought deductively to follow from premises 1–3. The first premise is something that seems reasonably to follow from the work of anthropologists. It is an empirical claim. But suppose someone rejected both the goals and methodology of anthropology and disputed premise 1 in the following way: Premise 1 is something that *you* ought to believe because it is established within the methodological framework of your own discipline. However, we outside of your discipline need not be forced to accept the truth of premise 1. We believe that such premises *ought not* be believed given our standards of what is rationally acceptable. Thus, if the conclusion of the argument is true that ethics is culturally relative, then the first premise of the argument ought only be believed by those who accept the epistemic framework of those making the attempt to establish premise 1 as true. Thus, if the conclusion of the argument for relativism is true, it undermines the possibility of any of the other premises being true. That is, the claim that we ought to believe that ethics are relative to culture cannot be established in a non-relativistic way, but clearly someone making the argument that ethics are relative to culture is stating more than the fact that they believe, given their own discipline's methodology that ethics are relative to culture. To sum up, if it turns out that ethics are relative to culture (i.e. all 'oughts' are nothing more than culturally determined practices) then the conclusion of this argument is only going to be something that ought to be believed by those within the culture (whatever that turns out to be) of the person(s) making the argument. But the conclusion of this type of relativistic argument is meant to persuade you that you *ought* to believe the conclusion, regardless of whether you are part of the cultural milieu of the person presenting the argument.

Some might quibble with the distinction between logical *oughts* and moral *oughts*. I may be begging the question here that the two are not merely analogous, but are in fact variants of one another. Here's a way to get at this idea. Suppose on an introductory logic exam a student claims that in standard Aristotelian categorical logic, a universal affirmative *A* claim, *All S are P* does NOT contradict the particular negative *O* claim, *Some S are not P*. Was this a *good* answer? It certainly wasn't logically good. The two are straightforwardly logically contradictory. But was it a morally bad answer too? Suppose the *A* and *O* claims show up in the following way: All acts of drinking eight litres of diesel fuel in 15 minutes or less are bad for your health, and Some acts of drinking eight gallons of diesel fuel in 15 minutes or less are not bad for your health. It seems that any student who believed the *A* claim and couldn't recognize that the corresponding *O* claim was a bad way to go about one's life, wouldn't be living the *good life* in any sense after drinking that much diesel fuel. Everything that we ought to believe in logic can contain propositions that apply directly to how we ought to live our lives. Further, there is a kind of moral precondition to doing logic as it is formally presented, a willingness to recognize that one simply cannot believe whatever one wants to believe; we ought to believe some things and not others in order to be and do well.

The Faulty Move from Descriptive to Prescriptive Relativism

In addition to the self-defeating nature of ethical (and all forms of) relativism, this particular argument for relativism hinges upon a faulty implication from the fact that cultures differ in their beliefs about ethics to the idea that there are no objective (i.e. non-relative) ethical truths. James Rachels has pointed this out rather nicely in his introductory book, *The Elements of Morality*.

The argument for ethical relativism goes something like this:

1. Cultures differ in their moral beliefs (some kill for affronts to their dignity, others don't).
2. If cultures differ in their moral beliefs, there are no objective (i.e. non-culturally relative) moral truths.
3. Thus, from 1 to 2, there are no objective moral truths.

The argument for ethical relativism might be applied to another intellectual discipline like, let's say, geography producing a similar argument:

1*. Cultures differ in their geographical beliefs (some think the earth is flat, others don't).
2*. If cultures differ in their geographical beliefs, there are no objective (i.e. non-culturally relative) geographical truths.
3*. Thus, from 1 to 2, there are no objective geographical truths.

The problem with the geographical argument is that it implies that a mere difference in ethical beliefs can imply that there are no truths to geography. This is quite similar to a case of a group of people riding a bus on a long road trip. Suppose half the bus believes that there is enough petrol in the tank to make it to their destination, and the other half does not believe that there is enough petrol to make it. Does the fact that the riders on the bus differ in their beliefs about petrol in the tank necessarily imply that there is no objective truth about there being petrol in the tank? Certainly not. So the idea behind this type of objection to cultural variance arguments put forth by Rachels is that merely believing something does not necessarily imply that there are no truths in that area of inquiry.

One possible rejoinder to this objection to the relativistic argument from cultural variance put forth by Rachels is that in terms of ordinary empirical beliefs such as how much petrol is in the tank, or what the shape of the earth might be, there are accessible and reasonable standards or methods by means of which we can settle disputes. One can, after all, sail around the world and come back to the point where one began, or one can insert a measuring stick into the petrol tank, drain the tank or drive until the bus stops running to find out how much petrol is in the tank. But in ethics, there just aren't these obvious scientific or empirical means that we can use to tell who is right in moral matters.

One might respond to this claim in several ways. First, the objection that there are no objective truths in ethics, but only in empirical matters is itself a philosophical claim and not an empirical claim. So, on this count if it is true, its truth cannot be found by simple empirical observation. Second, and more importantly, if one claims that there are no objective truths in ethics, but only in empirical matters, and one believes that everyone *ought* to believe this claim, then the claim is self-defeating.

The objection that there are no 'hard empirical facts' in ethics, like there are believed to be in disciplines such as physics or chemistry or engineering, cannot get off the ground simply by being asserted. One must first show, by way of argumentation, that there are no such moral truths. Oftentimes in discussing moral relativism with undergraduate students, we might compare how we would adjudicate an empirical dispute over the height of the administration building with how we would adjudicate a moral dispute over a case like the Kwakiutl mentioned above. Students will generally say something like, there are agreed-upon standards of how we measure height, so that in a dispute over the relation of 'taller than' between the administration building and the gymnasium, one could easily resolve the dispute by simply taking out a measuring device, a metre stick, and measuring the two buildings in order to compare which one is taller.[2] In ethics, students will often argue, there just isn't any objective measuring device (i.e. a moral stick) by means of which we can objectively measure two acts in order to see which one is morally better than the other, in the way that we can determine which building is physically higher than the other.[3]

The worry about a lack of a standard of moral measurement is a version of the notion of 'no neutrality' raised above, and it indeed is a large part of what motivates ethical relativism in the minds of students and reflective people generally. There are several ways to respond to this concern. One is simply to point out the self-defeating logical problem with ethical relativism. This I think shows that ethical relativism is unreasonable to maintain. However, pointing out that a position is unreasonable to maintain does not by itself provide a great deal of positive reasons to believe the contrary, i.e. that there are specific neutral standards of moral evaluation. I will suggest here a couple of strategies for thinking about such standards, and in Chapter 6 I will present a more formal argument for the possibility of neutral standards contrary to relativism.

First, one can simply read the history of ethics in order to see how great minds have dealt with the perennial questions about what the good life is all about, and who the good person is. In doing so, one will recognize that there have been really smart people across millennia who have rejected the idea that objective truths and neutral standards for judgement are limited solely to the empirical domain.

Second, one can attempt a positive defence of the existence of objective standards for ethical judgements. There is a long tradition of this type of defence of the objectivity of morality that is grounded in human nature itself and in our ability to see moral truths through or with our 'mind's eye'. Plato's *Republic*, Aristotle's *Nichomachean Ethics*, Augustine's *City of God*, Aquinas' *Summa*, Hume's *Treatise*, Kant's *Groundwork*, right up through Moore's *Principia* are just a few different ways of getting at this idea.

Third, one can point out the vast amount of commonality among moral traditions. (This is the third reason why the argument for relativism from moral variance should be rejected.) Such traditions differ in many ways: chronologically, religiously, geographically, culturally, linguistically, socially, economically, politically, ethnically, physically, etc. One such place to look for a very introductory account of the commonality of ethical beliefs is in the appendix to C.S. Lewis' little book *The Abolition of Man*. The three essays in this book attempt to defend the existence of objective moral standards (or what Lewis calls the *Tao*). At the end of the book, Lewis includes an appendix in order to illustrate, not prove (Lewis does not think that objective moral truths can be proved by means of a direct argument), the commonality of moral ideals across time, religion, culture, language, etc. Here are a few examples, which are quoted here directly from Lewis' text:

Law of General Beneficence
'slander not.' (Babylonian. *Hymn to Samas*. ERE v. 445)
'Thou shalt not bear false witness against thy neighbour.' (Ancient Jewish. Exodus 20:16)
'Utter not a word by which anyone could be wounded.' (Hindu. Janet, p. 7)

Duties to Children and Posterity
'Children, the old, the poor, etc. should be considered as lords of the atmosphere.' (Hindu. Janet, i. 8)
'Great reverence is owed to a child.' (Roman. Juvenal, xiv. 47)
'The Master said, Respect the young.' (Ancient Chinese. Analects, ix. 22)

Laws of Mercy
'Whoso makes intercession for the weak, well pleasing is this to Samas.' (Babylonian. ERE v. 445)
'I have given bread to the hungry, water to the thirsty, clothes to the naked, a ferry boat to the boatless.' (Ancient Egyptian. ERE v. 446)
'In the Dalebura tribe a woman, a cripple from birth, was carried about by the tribes-people in turn until her death at the age of sixty-six.'. . . 'They never desert the sick.' (Australian Aborigines. ERE v. 443)

Law of Magnanimity
'Is not the love of Wisdom a practice of death?' (Ancient Greek. Plato, Phadeo, 81 A)
'I know that I hung on the gallows for nine nights, wounded with the spear as a sacrifice to Odin, myself offered to Myself.' (Old Norse. Hávamál, I. 10 in Corpus Poeticum Boreale; stanza 139 in Hildebrand's Lieder der Älteren Edda. 1922)
'Verily, verily I say to you unless a grain of wheat falls into the earth and dies, it remains alone, but if it dies it bears much fruit. He who loves his life loses it.' (Christian. John 12:24,25) (Lewis 2001, pp. 83–103).

While these quotations do not amount to a proof for the objectivity of morality, they do provide reasons to reject a motivation for relativism, namely the idea that there are no common moral standards across cultures. Of course these similarities do not do away with the real differences in moral beliefs and practices, but do they militate against the idea that those differences must lead to relativism.

THE ARGUMENT FROM TOLERANCE

There is a second type of argument, an argument from the need for tolerance, which often motivates relativism. This type of argument has been less dominant in the philosophical literature as it is in popular culture. Here's one sort of minor example of this view from a recent kerfuffle in a California public school:

> A devout evangelical Christian, Chris [Niemeyer] wanted to give a commencement speech extolling the merits of Jesus . . . But school officials, wary of straying into the no-man's land separating church and state, broke with tradition and blocked the pair from addressing graduating classmates . . . 'To me, it's disrespectful when you ignore the diversity of your classmates and say you've got the only answer,' said Larry Payne, Oroville High School principal. 'I don't see God that way' (Bayley 1999, p. 1).

Whether or not there should be commencement speeches supporting particularly religious ideology, the claim by the principal seems to exemplify the kind of relativism that is based on the idea of tolerance. There are possibly three arguments that can be inferred from what the principal states:

Argument 1 (A1)

1.1 I believe that asserting a specific religious ideology is disrespectful to students who do not share the ideology.
1.2 Since I believe 1.1, then the speech should not be given.
1.3 Thus, the speech should not be given.

Argument 2 (A2)

2.1 I don't believe God would want a student to give a speech asserting a specific religious ideology disrespectful to students who do not share that ideology.

2.2 Since I believe 2.1, then the speech should not be given.

2.3 Thus, the speech should not be given.

Argument 3 (A3)

3.1 There is a great amount of religious diversity amongst the student body.

3.2 Given 3.1, if a speech contradicts the religious beliefs of another student, then it should not be given.

3.3 The speech will contradict the religious beliefs of another student.

3.4 Thus, the speech should not be given.

A1 and A2 are motivated by particular beliefs held by the principal. In A1 the key premise is the moral belief that asserting a specific religious ideology is bad. The challenge here is that asserting premise 1.1 may contradict the religious belief of a particular student. Then 1.3 does not follow. Even worse, in A2 premise 2.1 is a *theological* belief in which the principal's belief about God's character is invoked in order to justify a particularly religious belief. The ironic thing here is that this theological belief is believed by the principal appropriately to justify limitation of speech about theological matters. Can one have it both ways?

A3 is a bit different from A1 and A2 as it does not appeal to a particular belief held by the principal regarding the moral or theological grounds for prohibiting the student's speech. Rather, A3 appeals to the fact of descriptive relativism in public education (3.1). Premise 3.3 is a fact of the valedictorian's speech; it very well may contradict some students' religious beliefs. The key premise in this argument is 3.2. Asserting premise 3.2 requires a rejection of ethical relativism. One simply cannot be an ethical relativist and believe 3.2. In addition, suppose 3.2 is the type of speech that offensively contradicts a student's religious beliefs. Then it should not be given, and thus A3 must be rejected as well.

Arguments for relativism based on tolerance also show up in discussions with undergraduate students. Here are three examples from a few of my students in an introduction to ethics course a few years ago when I asked them to discuss relativism and objectivity about ethics:

Student 1: All attitudes towards individuals are personal, and the view of what the universe is, usually is culturally influenced. Some people believe they're right in one way, such as 'ProChoice' for women, whereas others view such people as 'murderers' (ProLife). It's all relative to the individual.

Student 2: Life is like an empty glass or container. There is nothing in the world. We fill this glass with our (a community of people) beliefs, moral values, etc. There should be a straight moral truth, but show me evidence of it! And what about different cultures; do we condemn them for not acting like ourselves? Why take the position of a sanctimonious ass-hole and condemn others? What do we do to other cultures that do not exercise the moral truth?

Student 3: Morals and behaviour vary through cultures. No one is to say which of these cultures are right or wrong, and therefore, no way of acting or casting judgement can be entirely right or wrong. While every person has a sense of what is true or false, this varies for every individual, with no one holding the power to correct another's perception of the world.

All three of these students are expressing a form of moral relativism. Students 2 and 3 are especially hinting at the idea that moral judgement from one party to another is not the type of thing that ought to be done. Regardless of the fact that saying, 'You shouldn't push your morality on someone else' is in fact a pushing of morality on one person by another (just another example of how relativism can be self-defeating), there is something amiss with the claim that tolerance can or should be a basis for ethical relativism.

We might be able to distinguish two types of tolerance: political tolerance (PT) and moral tolerance (MT). Political tolerance might be thought of as the idea that in a pluralistic culture and 'global village' there must be tolerance of different opinions, beliefs, practices and views at the level of political or societal interaction. Political tolerance is something that can be extended to all members of a liberal democracy, for example, under the aegis of a constitutional authority. PT, however, is often conflated with MT, where MT is the ethically relativistic view that there are no neutral moral standards by means of which to adjudicate between competing moral beliefs or practices. Students among others often believe that, since we want PT, we should advocate MT. The problem is that PT is not even possible without MT. If MT were true, then the type of political environment, say a Western liberal democracy, where PT could flourish, would be no better than a political environment, say a religious fundamentalist theocracy, which is something the advocate of PT would want to deny. So, PT is dependent on a rejection of MT rather than flowing from it. Pointing this out helps us realize that the type of political tolerance enjoyed in most universities in Western liberal democracies is one virtue among many that is only possible when ethical relativism is rejected.

THE 'UNLIVEABILITY' OF ETHICAL RELATIVISM

Even if it were possible for the logical self-contradiction of moral relativism to be resolved, and if it were possible to have a sound argument for relativism from cultural moral variance or from our need for tolerance, relativism would still be problematic in a practical way. Moral relativism simply cannot be lived out consistently. Any attempt to do so produces various absurdities. James Rachels, in his introduction to relativism in *The Elements of Morality* (Rachels 2007), points out three consequences of ethical relativism:

1. We can't say that some cultures' practices are morally better or worse. But can't we? Child abuse, slavery, oppression of women . . . these are things that are recognized in western liberal democracies as being morally wrong. If ethical relativism were true, and if these practices are thought to be good elsewhere, we cannot say that we are better off without them. But this seems absurd.
2. The rightness of our actions could be found 'by consulting the standards of our culture' (Rachels, p. 21). Thus, the commandants at Auschwitz who were following orders, given the standards of Nazi culture, were simply doing what was right, for them. But this runs against the intuition that merely going along with one's cultural practices does not absolve someone from their immoral actions.
3. We cannot make moral progress. Aren't there moral heroes today? Mother Teresa, Ghandi, Martin Luther King Jr. among others. If ethical relativism is true, then these heroes were actually doing what was immoral, given that they acted

contrary to the general moral ethos of the cultures in which they found themselves. Again, this just seems absurd, and thus we have a practical reason to reject moral relativism.[4]

CONCLUSION

Ethical relativism, although arising from a cultural milieu that is positively pluralistic, brings with it, once it moves from the descriptive to the prescriptive forms, a whole host of intellectual difficulties. First, it is self-defeating. Second, it rests on a shaky argument that unreasonably moves from the fact that cultures differ to the belief that there are no moral truths. Third, the argument from tolerance, while based on desirable ideas of political tolerance, does not justify the kind of morally relativistic tolerance that people often have in mind when they argue in this way. Fourth, there is a great deal of moral agreement, even in a pluralistic global village, and this undermines a motive for relativistic beliefs about morality. Last, ethical relativism is simply unliveable, and thus it should be rejected.

CHAPTER 5

AESTHETIC RELATIVISM

INTRODUCTION

The phrase 'Beauty is in the eye of the beholder' is common enough. With works of art, some people like the classical paintings of Michelangelo, some people like the impressionism of Monet, some people like the abstract paintings of Pollock. With music, some people like Gregorian chant, other people like Bach, and still others like Metallica. With human beings, one person finds another person exceedingly beautiful, while someone else thinks that same person is average looking or plain ugly. There is so much diversity of taste in the realm of aesthetics, of what people believe is ugly or beautiful, that this seems to imply that *being beautiful* or beauty itself is simply relative to a person's own preference or desire.

This fact of diversity of taste is analogous to the descriptive moral relativism presented in Chapter 3. This fact has been called by Nicholas Davey, 'pragmatic aesthetic relativism' which in part 'simply recognizes the *de facto* existence of a plurality of modes of appreciation and idioms of truth claim, not only in a culture but also between cultures' (Davey 1992, p. 358). However, Davey's 'pragmatic aesthetic relativism' goes beyond the notion of merely describing the differences in the standards of judgement used in both identifying and evaluating works of art. This type of relativism seems to deny the possibility of a 'universal foundation' for all aesthetic judgements. Such a denial could be a version of accepting the no-neutrality conjunct in the description of relativism given in previous chapters, and in this case specifically denying the idea that there are any neutral standards by means of which to judge disputes about what is or is not beautiful.

However, it is not clear from Davey's description of this version of aesthetic relativism if such a denial must be put forward by this pragmatic position. Davey states, 'Pragmatic relativism . . . is consistent with appeals to intersubjective criteria for aesthetic appraisals within distinct aesthetic communities' (p. 358). Problems arise, according to Davey, when one tries to argue for the position of pragmatic relativism, as it 'cannot simultaneously declare itself to be *the* most appropriate way of looking at the arts *and* advocate plurality of interpretive values' (p. 359).[1] It seems to me that with pragmatic aesthetic relativism, as long as it serves as a cautious reminder that there are many different standards of evaluation of works of art, and natural objects for their aesthetic qualities, there is no logical problem. John Hyman offers us this type of descriptivist or pragmatic aesthetic relativistic reminder:

Relativism is the simplest alternative to the monistic idea that there is a single model of truth and perfection in the visual arts, and it has generally been accepted for this reason.[2] Relativists deplore the provincialism that makes European art seem to embody all of the timeless truths about what art should be. They know how our perceptions can be dulled and our sympathies narrowed by an exclusive attachment to the methods and techniques which our own artistic tradition has inherited. They know that societies have used art for different purposes, and to express ideas of very different kinds. They know that the values embodied in art and demanded in criticism in a particular place and time are not more valid because they resemble our own. And they know that what looks like technical progress from one point of view can look like decline into empty virtuosity from another (Hyman 2004, p. 50).

A more problematic version of aesthetic relativism, analogous to prescriptive ethical relativism, is what Davey calls,

Dogmatic relativism, which denies either the existence or the knowability of ahistorical, universal or eternal truths about art's alleged intrinsic nature or the qualities of aesthetic appreciation, concluding that all truth claims about art and our modes of understanding it are unverifiable and, consequently, equivalent to each other (Davey 1992, p. 357).

What might motivate such a position? There may be two types of argument for relativism about beauty. The first type of argument is an argument from the non-existence of objective aesthetic properties. In fact, James Young defines relativism *vis-à-vis* aesthetic realism which maintains the existence of objective aesthetic properties. Young states,

> Relativism is best understood in opposition to aesthetic realism. According to aesthetic realism, any sentence expressing a judgment about the aesthetic value of an artwork is true if and only if the artwork possesses certain properties. The aesthetic realist holds that if a work of art possesses these properties, then not only is the judgment that it is valuable true, but any contrary judgment is false. The aesthetic realist further holds that critics' feelings and beliefs about a work of art have nothing to do with the truth values of judgments about its aesthetic value. Aesthetic relativism, on the other hand, is the view that the truth values of sentences which express judgments about the aesthetic values of artworks are not determined by the objective features of the artworks. Instead, the truth values of such sentences depend, at least in part, on the critics who make the judgments (Young 1997, p. 10).[3]

This type of argument attempts to show that aesthetic properties like beauty and ugliness aren't *really* properties *in* objects. Physical properties (height, weight, volume) are *really in* objects, but aesthetic properties aren't; they are in the mind of the individual aesthetically evaluating these objects, and thus they are relative to those judgements or evaluations.

In addition to an argument from the subjectivity of aesthetic properties, there is a second type of argument for aesthetic relativism. This is an argument from aesthetic diversity, similar to the same type of argument for ethical relativism. This type of argument tries to move from premises regarding both the amount and the depth of differences in aesthetic preferences and tastes to the conclusion that beauty is nothing more than those preferences; beauty is relative to taste.

There seems to be an important relationship between these two arguments. The argument from aesthetic diversity seems to depend on the argument from aesthetic subjectivism. If one can demonstrate that aesthetic qualities aren't really in objects, but rather in the subjective feelings of perceivers, then argumentation about whether something is beautiful or not becomes pointless. We can argue about how tall a building is. Just get out the metre stick, because height is objective. It's really in the building. But we can't argue about whether the building is ugly, because ugliness is in the mind of the perceiver of the building, not in the building. There's no 'ugly stick' that we can use to tell whether the building is ugly. The building's being ugly is relative to your own individual preference. This argument bolsters the argument from aesthetic diversity by helping to explain it. Why are there so many different preferences about beauty? Well, you know, beauty is nothing more than personal taste. Since there are so many different tastes, beauty is relative to those tastes. Let us examine each of these arguments in turn.

THE ARGUMENT FROM THE SUBJECTIVITY OF AESTHETIC PROPERTIES

C.S. Lewis, in the first chapter of *The Abolition of Man*, provides a nice, short and accessible summary of both a statement and a brief refutation of the argument from subjectivity for the relativity of aesthetic properties. In this chapter, Lewis wants to show that both aesthetic and ethical relativism are problematic. He begins with a discussion of aesthetic relativism in which he presents a relativistic argument *for* aesthetic relativism, and then provides a refutation of this argument. I've given a rather lengthy quotation of this passage below. First the statement of the relativistic argument:

In their second chapter Gaius and Titius [Two pseudonyms for real authors who have written a high school English grammar textbook] quote the well-known story of Coleridge at the waterfall. You remember that there were two tourists present: that one called it 'sublime' and the other 'pretty'; and that Coleridge mentally endorsed the first judgement and rejected the second with disgust. Gaius and Titius comment as follows: 'When the man said *This is sublime*, he appeared to be making a remark about the waterfall . . . Actually . . . he was not making a remark about the waterfall, but a remark about his own feelings. What he was saying was really '*I have feelings associated in my mind with the word "Sublime"*, or shortly, "*I have sublime feelings*" '. Here are a good many deep questions settled in a pretty summary fashion.

But the authors are not yet finished. They add: 'This confusion is continually present in language as we use it. We appear to be saying something very important about something: and actually we are only saying something about our own feelings' (Lewis 2001, pp. 3–4).

We can formalize this aesthetic relativistic argument as follows:

Abbreviations:

S an individual subject
A an aesthetic property
O an object of experience
F a feeling of a property

Argument:

P1: S has a visual experience of O that produces F of P in S.
P3: Therefore, A is nothing more than F.

This isn't a very good argument, logically good that is. From the fact that S experiences O and has a feeling of P, why should we think that P is nothing other than F in S? David Hume (1711–76) offers a better argument for this position in his little essay 'On the Standard of Taste' (Hume 1965), which takes the form of a *reductio ad absurdum*.[4]

Before coming to the argument, Hume is careful to distinguish between what he calls judgement and sentiment. On the one hand, human beings make judgements which come from the understanding (i.e. the logical operations of reason in the mind). Not all judgements that people have are correct. Some judgements are true, and others are false. According to Hume, this is because judgements refer to something beyond themselves, which Hume calls 'matters of fact'. When judgements differ between people, 'there is one, and but one, that is just and true' (p. 6). Logical or mathematic relations or scientific, empirical observations would fit in this category.

On the other hand, all sentiments are always 'right'. Sentiments refer to nothing beyond themselves. Hume states,

a thousand different sentiments, excited by the same object, are all right; because no sentiment represents what is really in the object. It only marks a certain conformity or relation between the object and the organs or faculties of the mind and if that conformity did not really exist, the sentiment could never possibly have being (p. 6).

With this distinction in mind, we can reconstruct Hume's argument:

    i. Objects that taste sweet are sweet (i.e. have the property of being sweet in them).

    ii. 'According to the dispositions of the organs [e.g. the tongue], the same object may be both sweet and bitter' (p. 6).

    iii. No object can have contradictory properties simultaneously (e.g. sweet and not sweet).

    iv. Therefore, objects don't have properties of taste in them.

    v. Therefore, i. is false.

    vi. Aesthetic responses of beauty occurring in the mind are analogous to taste responses occurring in the tongue.

    vii. No object can have contradictory properties simultaneously (e.g. beauty and not-beauty).

    viii. Therefore, objects don't have beauty in them.

This reconstructed argument seems to capture the general sentiment of Gaius and Titius, the authors Lewis is arguing against in *The Abolition of Man*. This position rejects the objectivity of beauty in that it claims that there aren't properties of being beautiful or being ugly that are actually in objects, rather these are properties (or relations) that obtain between perceivers and things perceived. This position, the denial of aesthetic properties being in objects, need not lead to relativism where relativism here is understood as the idea that all works of art or natural objects can be equally beautiful just in case they are believed to be beautiful by persons who perceive them. Hume is very careful to deny this relativistic position.

Hume denies that aesthetic standards are 'fixed by reasonings *a priori*' (p. 7). There aren't transcendental non-human-nature-based standards for evaluating objects for their aesthetic qualities. Hume does claim that experience tells us, nearly universally, what pleases us aesthetically and this is based 'on the observation of the common sentiments of human nature' (p. 8). For Hume, great beautiful works of art 'are naturally fitted to excite agreeable sentiments, immediately display their energy: and while the world endures, they maintain their authority over the minds of men' (p. 9); adding further

'Though it be certain that beauty and deformity, more than sweet and bitter, are not qualities in objects, but belong entirely to the sentiment, internal or external, it must be allowed, that there are certain qualities in objects, which are fitted by nature to produce those particular feelings' (p. 11). Hume does maintain that we can know beautiful and ugly things through practice and training of our aesthetic sense organs (pp. 11–13). Lastly, he is very careful to deny any sort of simplistic relativism. He states, 'It is sufficient for our present purpose, if we have proved that the taste of all individuals is not upon equal footing' (p. 18).

The trouble, it seems to me, with Hume's argument is that if aesthetic properties aren't really in objects, but are merely in the individual's sentiments, which are part of one's constituent human nature, and if there are general standards that point to the idea that not all tastes are on equal footing, then one must show how it is that not all tastes are on equal footing contrary to the relativistic view that denies this. So, Hume has a general argument that not all tastes are on an equal footing, an argument that relies on near-universal approbation of certain literary works, test of time, endurance, etc. However, if a relativist claims that this argument (which certainly isn't entirely *a priori*) does not produce in her the taste of approbation, what is Hume to do? He can appeal to common acceptance of such an argument, but he cannot logically show that disagreement with his own position, if it is one based on taste, is inferior to his own view. Thus, the shift from a denial of the objectivity of aesthetic properties leads subtly to relativism about those properties.

Let us return now to Lewis' rejoinder to the objections to the objectivity of beauty raised by Gaius and Titius. Lewis says that there are two reasons we should reject Gaius and Titius' views. First, even if aesthetic properties aren't in objects, but are mere mental projections (or Humean sentiments), the properties projected have to be different from the feelings that I have about the object. Second, identifying aesthetic properties with personal feelings leads to absurdities. Here's a long quotation from Lewis to see his point:

Before considering the issues really raised by this momentous little paragraph (designed, you will remember, for 'the upper forms of schools') we must eliminate one mere confusion into which Gaius and Titius have fallen. Even on their own view – on any conceivable view – the man who says *This is sublime* cannot mean *I have sublime feelings*. Even if it were granted that such qualities as sublimity were simply and solely projected into things from our own emotions, yet the emotions which prompt the projection are the correlatives, and therefore almost the opposites, of the qualities projected. The feelings which make a man call an object sublime are not sublime feelings but feelings of veneration. If *This is sublime* is to be reduced at all to a statement about the speaker's feelings, the proper translation would be *I have humble feelings*. If the view held by Gaius and Titius were consistently applied it would lead to obvious absurdities. It would force them to maintain that *You are contemptible* means *I have contemptible feelings*, in fact that *Your feelings are contemptible* means *My feelings are contemptible* (Lewis 2001, p. 4).

The main point of Lewis' first argument is that even if we grant (which Lewis himself does not) that aesthetic properties are nothing more than feelings, our feelings are not the same as the properties projected. For example, if I'm standing in the desert on a dark, cloudless, moonless night with excellent visibility of the sky, and I see the Milky Way and all the constellations above me, and I declare, 'This is awesome', I am not feeling awesome, or vast or infinite. I'm feeling rather small, insignificant and finite. The emotions we have are not the same as the properties we project onto objects, if in fact aesthetic properties are nothing more than projections of our sentimental faculties.

The main point of Lewis' second argument is that the reduction of aesthetic properties to feelings leads to absurdities. For example, if I say, 'You're ugly', that means I have ugly feelings, which implies that somehow *I'm* ugly. But, when I say 'You're ugly', I certainly don't mean to assert that '*I'm* ugly' too! (Although I may very well be!) These considerations should be enough to militate against the idea that aesthetic properties can be easily reduced to emotional states on the grounds that this idea has serious logical difficulties.

AN ARGUMENT FROM AESTHETIC DIVERSITY

In addition to arguments from the subjectivity of aesthetic properties, there are some motivations for aesthetic relativism which come from the fact that both individuals and groups of people differ, sometimes greatly, over what counts as being beautiful or ugly. Joseph Margolis presents one such argument for 'a relativistic conception of aesthetic appreciation' (Margolis 1987, p. 495), which makes use of the facts of aesthetic diversity.

Margolis' argument rests on two considerations:

1. 'Works of art are . . . culturally emergent entities [which are] notoriously open to intensional quarrels . . . and there is no obvious way in which to show that . . . incompatible characterizations of cultural items can be sorted as correct or incorrect in such a way that a relativistic account would be precluded' (p. 495).
2. Values themselves are non-cognitive, as human persons are 'culturally emergent entities . . . Consequently, the prospects of avoiding a relativistic account of values (and of value judgments) . . . is nearly nil' (p. 496).

It seems to me that Margolis' first point is simply a restatement of the general argument for relativism considered in Chapter 1. Margolis claims first that there are standards of evaluations of works of art which arise from within a culture. Second, there is no neutrality between competing standards of evaluation. Thus, relativism follows.

In Chapter 2 we argued that a generalization of relativism about knowledge along these lines was problematic because it is self-defeating. Can a similar argument be placed here? Is it self-defeating to maintain both that works of art, or natural entities, are judged to be beautiful only by some standard of aesthetic evaluation, and further that there is no neutrality between standards of evaluation? I presented the following simplified argument against epistemic relativism above:

1. If there is a standard by which ER (epistemological relativism) is judged to be false, then ER is false.
2. There is a standard by which ER is judged to be false.
3. Therefore, ER is false.

This argument seems to work when referring to knowledge claims, since the relativistic position about knowledge seems to require a neutral position if it is going to be asserted at all. But does an argument for aesthetic relativism make such a mistake as well?

1. If there is a standard by which AR (aesthetic relativism) is judged to be false, then AR is false.
2. There is a standard by which AR is judged to be false.
3. Therefore, AR is false.

The problem with this argument is that AR is about aesthetics, not particularly about knowledge, and in premise 2, the standard appealed to here by means of which AR is judged to be false would be an *epistemic* standard and not an aesthetic one. So this argument, on the face of it, is unsound.

There might be two ways to avoid this problem. One way would be to collapse AR into ER, by showing that AR is a species of ER, with claims about knowledge applied only to the limited realm of our knowledge of beauty. So, if this can be done, then the standards by which AR is judged to be false are simply epistemic standards applied to the realm of aesthetics. Thus, the argument is sound, as AR is simply a limit case of ER.

The second way to avoid this problem is to argue that any argument for AR itself contains an aesthetic element that is itself immune from the relativist's claim. This seems like an odd thing to do, i.e. to posit that arguments themselves have aesthetic elements in them which, contrary to the relativistic claim, are thought to be beautiful in a neutral way. This is to say that any relativistic argument for aesthetic relativism would either have contained within it, as a work of art (if arguments can be works of art), a property of being lovely (elegance is often used as an aesthetic quality in mathematics) or beautiful, or it would not. If such an argument were elegant, then of course the relativistic position would have to be abandoned. If such an argument weren't elegant, then well, if elegance is a condition for the goodness of an argument or a position to hold, the relativist's position would be weakened.

These considerations point to the possibility of the interconnectivity of the aesthetic with the epistemic. The ideas presented here seem to be a bit tendentious, and possibly need to be fleshed out in more detail. Suffice it for now to say that if the rational persuasiveness of an argument depends on any aesthetic property within it, any argument for aesthetic relativism would be inconsistent.[5]

Let us return to Margolis' second point raised above. This second point is that values themselves are non-cognitive. The idea of values being non-cognitive means generally that values themselves do not exist in objects (see the discussion of Hume above), and that value judgements are neither cognitively true nor false. There are a variety of non-cognitive positions about values (emotivism, prescriptivism, etc.). It is beyond the scope of this book to sort out the details of these various positions. Let us instead consider what Margolis' claim amounts to.

Margolis claims that since values themselves are non-cognitive, then relativism follows. The question that immediately comes to mind is this: Is his position a good one to believe? The term 'good' in this question might be ambiguous between epistemically good and axiologically good.[6] If Margolis' claim is 'good' to believe in the former sense, then it will likely need to be based on good (i.e. reasonable) arguments for the position. This, of course, would require a full examination of the evidence for and against non-cognitivism. But suppose that non-cognitivism about values is in fact epistemically good to believe, i.e. the evidence for non-cognitivism is better than its competitors. Would then maintaining non-cognitivism be axiologically good to believe? If the relativist says, 'Yes' then the relativist is maintaining something contrary to her own position, that values are non-cognitive. The relativist might respond that she only means that the relativistic position is non-cognitive, and that the anti-relativistic position which maintains that non-cognitivism is not axiologically good to believe is equally axiologically good as the relativistic position. Thus, the relativist would have to believe that her own position was axiologically as good as a *rejection* of her own position. This seems absurd, as it entails that one ought to reject the relativist's own position on axiological grounds, which seems to be something that a relativist would deny. So, Margolis' second point, in addition to requiring a strong argument in favour of non-cognitivism, seems to lead to an absurd position in which the relativism that non-cognitivism supposedly entails is both axiologically good and axiologically bad.

CONCLUSION

Once again, this is one of the main problems of relativism. In art or in ontology, universal generalizations denying the possibility of existence or reality are self-defeating. Thus relativism in aesthetics should be rejected. Such a rejection does not tell us which natural objects or works of art are beautiful or ugly, it merely opens at least the possibility of there being such aesthetic realities.

CHAPTER 6

RELATIVISTIC WORLDVIEWS IN SCIENCE, POLITICS AND RELIGION, AND THE POSSIBILITY OF NEUTRALITY

INTRODUCTION

The four main areas of philosophy (ontology, epistemology, ethics and aesthetics) deal with the most general categories for all areas of human inquiry. Anything that the human mind can study, from cars to carcinogens, from the tango to time, will be something real (which is the domain of ontology), knowable (epistemology), and good (ethics and aesthetics). This is one of the attractions of studying philosophy. It intrudes into all other disciplines in the academy and beyond. Relativism as a general account of reality, knowledge, morality or beauty will thus have implications in any and all areas of human inquiry that deal with any one or more of these transcendentals of philosophy.

I've selected three topics in this chapter to deal with: science, politics and religion. The first deals with relativism in science. We examine some of the major thoughts and ideas of Thomas Kuhn, whose ideas of 'paradigms' in the history of science have contributed to a powerful way of thinking about how scientific advancements are actually made and the nature of scientific inquiry itself. I've selected this particular topic in order to show that even the area of human inquiry most often thought to be immune from relativistic thinking has come under its influence in recent years.

The second topic is relativism in political theory. This section deals not so much with political philosophy as such, but rather examines one recent conception of political thought in the philosophy of Alasdair MacIntyre in order to show how relativism in epistemology militates against a coherent political philosophy. The third and final topic covers relativism in religion. Again, as I am not an expert in the study of religions, I will simply consider what implications relativism might have on interactions within and between religions in specific areas of religious belief such as heresy and blasphemy.

In the final section of the chapter, I will introduce the idea of how we can have neutrality between competing understandings of standards of evaluation of philosophical claims. This idea of establishing neutrality between competing standards of evaluation applies to conflicts between competing standards of evaluation in all areas where relativism is thought to be the inevitable outcome of such conflicts. I will argue that relativism is *not* the inevitable outcome of conflicts between competing standards of evaluation, but rather given that we have standards of evaluation at all, such a resolution of conflicting standards is a real possibility. This of course does not tell us which side to believe in such a conflict, but it does allow such conflicts to be resolvable in principle. This idea of coming to have neutral standards of evaluation will be applicable to all of the areas of relativism treated in this book whether in ontology, epistemology, ethics or aesthetics.

FURTHER ELABORATION OF THE CONCEPT OF STANDARDS OF EVALUATION AS 'WORLDVIEWS'

Before we examine relativism in its application to specific disciplines, I would like to say something about the concept of 'worldview' (e.g. scientific worldview, religious worldview, political worldview) and discuss how it relates to our discussion of relativism. The notion of worldview can be used as a general substitute for something like the standards conjunct in the definition of relativism used above. One's worldview might be that by means of which one determines whether a particular belief is justified or rationally acceptable. However, there are a few different concepts of the concept of 'worldview' and in this section I would like to present those concepts and show that when the concept of worldview is rightly understood, it allows one to avoid the difficulties of epistemic relativism raised above.

How might the concept of worldview be helpful for scholars? Let me answer this question by starting with three recent definitions of worldview:

Worldview = def:

a. 'A worldview is a commitment, a fundamental orientation of the heart, that can be expressed as a story or in a set of presuppositions . . . which we hold . . . about the basic constitution of reality, and that provides the foundation on which we live and move and have our being' (Sire 2004, p. 122).

b. 'A worldview is best understood as a semiotic phenomenon, especially as a system of narrative signs that establishes a powerful framework within which people think (reason), interpret (hermeneutics), and know (epistemology)' (Naugle 2003, p. xix).

c. 'Philosophy can help someone form a rationally justified, true worldview, that is, an ordered set of propositions about life's most important questions' (Craig and Moreland 2003, p. 13).

I think that there are at least three ideas that can be derived from these definitions of worldview that might be helpful for scholars. (1) Worldviews consist of mental states that are about what is real. Whether these mental states are merely presuppositions or beliefs that are the result of evidences from thought or experience, these definitions indicate that a coherent concept of worldview consists of beliefs about the world. These beliefs are parts of a larger mental 'map' that is used by the person who has it to develop an understanding of the nature of reality. (2) These definitions have something important to say about the practical implications of worldviews. A worldview helps one deal with reality, helps one move through the world, and contains directional information about how one should live one's life. (3) Worldviews can either be true or false. If the concept of worldview is to be helpful for thought and life, it must contain within it the notion that worldviews can be true or false, and because they are true or false, there are better and worse worldviews (just as there are better and worse maps or sets of directions to get one from Miami to Los Angeles). Presuppositions can either reflect or not reflect the world; narrative signs can either point us in the right direction or in the wrong direction; propositions can either correspond or not correspond to reality. Part of my worry is that a concept of worldview that either minimizes or entirely neglects this third component will not only fail to be coherent, but will also fail to do any intellectual work at all.

I have two major worries with the general notions of worldview as defined above. The first is from Kant (and both his empiricist and rationalist predecessors). Kant appears to be the first major philosopher to use the notion of worldview. My worry here is essentially a worry about what these definitions of worldview listed above mean by the crucial notions of 'commitments', 'narrative signs' or 'propositions'. If one's understanding of these notions involves the idea that these entities either (a) stand between me and the world[1] (so that I don't know the world as it is, but only my 'ideas' or 'signs' or 'propositions' or 'presuppositions'),[2] or (b) construct or shape reality, because they stand between reality and me, then I think we *must* reject them. For example, if Naugle's semiotic structures stand between us and the world in such a way that I am only aware of the signs and not the world, then I believe that this is problematic, but if Naugle's semiotic structures simply give us direction or give meaning to that in the world which we immediately know, then I believe that this is un-problematic, but still in need of a realistic ontological and epistemological grounding.

I believe that a correct understanding of the concept of worldview cannot and must not include any notion that one's worldview stands between them and reality or shapes, constructs, or makes (even in part) reality for the person. Any understanding of the concept of worldview *logically* cannot include the notion that one's worldview stands between them and the world and constructs their experiences. If one were to claim this, one would essentially be claiming that one *knows* the nature of one bit of reality, namely 'that worldviews stand between me and reality' and either one knows this because one has got at that bit of reality as it is in itself, or they have not. If they have, then it is not the case that worldviews stand between me and reality, but if they haven't then they don't know that bit of reality, namely 'that worldviews stand between me and reality'.

The logical problem is similar if one maintains that one's worldview shapes or constructs the world for a person. (This is the same general problem raised in our discussion of ontological relativism.) This type of epistemology has been called the 'Midas Touch Epistemology' (Willard 1993). It is the view that somehow the mind, or in our case worldviews as mental entities, affect (make, shape, construct, taint, etc.) in some way the world that we experience. This view is problematic. Things (desks, people, cars, God) being what they are could not be produced (given their characteristics) by a worldview being what it is. How could a worldview commitment of the heart or *qua* system of signs or *qua* set of propositions do anything to an object or give properties to an object? Worldviews, being what they are, and given the properties that they have can't possibly shape, construct or *do* anything to extra-mental reality given the properties that it has.

This may not be particularly convincing, if one does not think that worldviews literally do things to extra-mental reality, but the following argument should persuade those who maintain that worldviews condition reality for us. If things take their properties from worldviews (where a worldview consists in part in either properties of consciousness or language, e.g. presuppositions, systems of signs, or propositions) this will be because of, or due to, what worldviews *are*. If worldviews condition reality, it is because they are real and have unconditioned properties; but then reality is unconditioned. So, a concept of worldview, containing the notion that a worldview either stands between me and reality or conditions it, is logically problematic and should be rejected.

If we fail to reject the notion that one's worldview stands between one's mind and reality, or shapes reality, then this may lead to a self-defeating relativism, which looks something like this. We only have access to our worldviews, or our worldviews create the world for us, and so for any knowledge claim *p*, *p* can only be established by one's worldview, and given a different worldview there is no neutral way of choosing between the two worldviews. This is especially worrisome if Naugle is right that reason is grounded in worldview (Naugle, p. 310). That is, *p*'s truth or rational justification is relative to the worldview in which it is established. The arguments for and against this type of epistemically relativistic claim have been discussed in Chapter 2 above. We will not here rehearse those arguments; just suffice it to say that any attempts of this sort to get around the self-defeating nature of relativism do not appear promising.

My worry is that without a carefully articulated non-relativistic ontology and epistemology, the concept of 'worldview' defined in multiple ways above is both *too* modern and *too* post-modern. Without the correct ontology, the concept of worldview may contain the modern notion that (i) a worldview stands between me and reality, and two post-modern notions (ii) a worldview constructs reality for me, and (iii) given competing worldviews, there can be no non-neutral standards for adjudication, and thus relativism follows. So, if scholars, regardless of their field, are going to use the concept of worldview in any of the senses defined above, they should do so in ways that are directly realistic and thus non-relativistic.

How might someone make use of the concept of worldview that does not run afoul of either indirect realism, constructivism or relativism? Does doing this imply that we should maintain that we can have an understanding of reality that has 'objective, universal, and timeless validity' (Naugle, p. 119)? I believe that it does. One possible initial objection raised (and I think maintained) by Naugle is that any attempt to defend a philosophy that has 'objective, universal, and timeless validity' is to construct a presuppositionless view of the world. I'm not sure that this is right. That is, one can maintain the definitions of worldview above, and maintain that there is knowledge that is objective, universal and timelessly valid, without claiming that this is a presuppositionless philosophy. One could maintain that one's claim to have a worldview that is objective, universal and timelessly valid is a *worldview* (even as defined above). That claim isn't self-defeating, although it might be false.

Suppose someone did maintain p:

   p: I have knowledge that is independent of a worldview.

Suppose that p is self-defeating.[3] This implies that we can know q.

   q: Worldviews exist and have objective properties that can be known, one of which is that we can't have knowledge without them.

This implies r and s.

   r: Worldviews can't condition all of reality for us.

   s: There is knowledge that is objective, timeless and universally valid.

It seems to me that we cannot escape the logical point that there is knowledge that is objective, timeless and universally valid. Thus, the very concept of 'worldview' cannot be used to imply relativism. It is just the opposite; the concept of worldview implies non-relativism.

RELATIVISM AND SCIENCE: THE CASE OF THOMAS KUHN

Kuhn's notion of 'paradigm' (one way of understanding the concept of 'worldview') might fit the bill for the standards conjunct of the definition of relativism we've been using in this work. A paradigm is, according to Kuhn, a scientific achievement that has two features: i) it was successful enough in solving problems that it drew adherents away from competing modes of scientific activity and ii) it left a number of problems unsolved to be worked out by the new group of scientists (Kuhn 1996, p. 10). A paradigm in this sense may be a necessary condition for making scientific judgements much in the same way a standard of epistemic evaluation is used to justify/establish/make reasonable, etc., any type of belief. For example, Kuhn gives a case of a chemist and a physicist being asked whether 'a single atom of helium was or was not a molecule' (p. 50). The chemist from his paradigm answers 'yes', and the physicist from his answers 'no'. This seems to indicate that the answer to specific scientific questions is a matter of reference to a paradigm. This seems to be a case of the standards conjunct in our definition of relativism.

What about the no-neutrality conjunct? Does Kuhn maintain it? In his introduction to his chapter 'Revolutions as Changes of World View', Kuhn writes, 'The scientist can have no recourse to what he sees with his eyes and instruments. If there were some higher authority by recourse to which his vision might be shown to have shifted, then that authority would itself become his source of data . . .' (p. 114). This seems to be a denial of a kind of extra-paradigmatic standard for scientific judgement, i.e. no neutrality. Several other examples that Kuhn gives seem to point this way, such as the discovery of Uranus. Uranus was thought once to be a star, then a comet and finally a planet, and once it was recognized to be a planet, 'there were several fewer stars and one more planet in the world of the professional astronomer' (p. 115). This could be interpreted as a kind of ontological relativity in that the heavenly body we call 'Uranus' was once a star, was once a comet and now is a planet.[4] Kuhn uses the locution, 'though the world does not change with a change of paradigm, the scientist afterward works in a different world' (p. 121).

Does this amount to a denial of neutrality? Kuhn seems to equivocate on this point. On the one hand, he claims that he finds it 'impossible to relinquish' the notion of neutrality, but on the other hand, claims that 'it no longer functions effectively' (p. 126). He further states, 'No language thus restricted to reporting a world fully known in advance can produce mere neutral and objective reports on "the given"' (p. 127). These quotations seem to point to a rejection of neutrality between competing standards of the justification of scientific beliefs.

If Kuhn means his various examples to point to a strong rejection of the possibility of neutrality between competing paradigms, then it seems to me his views lead to a form of relativism that will be problematic in the same ways as the other forms of relativism considered above. However, Kuhn's denial of neutrality may only be a denial of 'global neutrality' (i.e. a denial that there is one fixed standard of neutrality that solves all disputes for all times). Kuhn may not be denying 'local neutrality' (i.e. the possibility of standards that can be had between particular competing standards of epistemic evaluation that occur in specific scientific disputes).

Consider an example from the history of science.[5] Ptolemaic astronomers attempted to establish proposition p,

p: The earth is the centre of planetary motion,
by means of the following standards of evaluation S_1:
  S_1: Conceptual economy, the ability to explain common-sense experiences, and understandability (Kuhn 1957, pp. 37–8).[6]
Copernican astronomers attempted to establish proposition q,
  q: The sun is the centre of planetary motion,
by means of a standard of evaluation S_2:
  S_2: Fruitfulness, i.e. 'the effectiveness [of theories] as guides for research and as frameworks for the organization of knowledge' (p. 40).

According to the relativist, given these different standards of evaluation, there is no neutral way to determine which standard to use, and thus there is no neutral way to establish p or q over and above the other. However, contrary to the relativist, the mere fact that S_1 and S_2 are different standards of evaluation means neither that there can be no neutrality between them nor that the propositions established by them cannot be established as superior to the other. Rather, it means that if each side understands their standards to be established for non-question-begging good reasons, then each side is committed to the possibility of local neutrality.

Kuhn indicates that each side in the dispute between Ptolemaic and Copernican views of astronomy[7] held their standards for what they took to be non-question-begging good reasons. One of the main reasons that each side maintained the standards they did included the ability of their standards of evaluation to 'solve the problems' of planetary motion. They took this reason to be non-question-begging and non-arbitrary. Ptolemaic astronomers thought that these problems were solvable by the addition of multiple epicycles. Copernicus thought that the Ptolemaic view was incompatible with (and simpler than) available observational data, and thus one of the reasons Copernicans rejected the Ptolemaic model was that it did not seem to solve the problems as well as the Copernican model.

According to Kuhn, Copernicans also held their standards for reasons of 'quantitative precision' (Kuhn 1962, p. 153) as a kind of problem-solving ability. Kuhn states, 'The quantitative superiority of Kepler's Rudolphine tables to all those computed from the Ptolemaic theory was a major factor in the conversion of astronomers to Copernicanism' (p. 154). Another example of what the Copernicans took to be non-question-begging good reasons for holding the standards that they held is shown in Kuhn's indication that Kepler's ability to use his mathematical models combined with the data of Tycho Brahe's observation allowed him to develop a simple mathematical technique that 'yielded predictions [of planetary motion] far more accurate than any that had ever been made before' (Kuhn 1957, p. 212). The Copernicans' commitments to non-arbitrary, good reasons for the standards that they had imply that they were committed to the possibility of locally neutral standards that could settle their dispute with the Ptolemaics.

This example shows that one can maintain the standards conjunct of relativism, and deny one type of neutrality, i.e. global neutrality, without the resultant problems of relativism raised above. In this account taken from Kuhn's work, no relativism entails, since there is no denial of local neutrality. The shift from a Ptolemaic to a Copernican astronomy was not an arbitrary relativist paradigm shift. It was one that was based upon non-arbitrary, good reasons for the standards that were held by the disputing parties. Thus, a resolution to the conflict could in principle be had, without a slide into a form of subjectivism or relativism.

In fact, in responding to various critics of his own views, Kuhn seems to maintain just this point: that there can be local neutrality between competing scientific paradigms. One critic of his views claims that Kuhn's apparent denial of neutrality leads to a kind of relativistic situation in which, '"the decision of a scientific group to adopt a new paradigm cannot be based on good reasons of any kind, factual or otherwise"' (Kuhn 1977, p. 321). Kuhn is careful to explain that there are characteristics, apparently neutral ones, that can be used as marks of good scientific theories. He lists five of them: accuracy, consistency, scope, simplicity, fruitfulness. Given such a list, one can hardly accuse Kuhn of relativism regarding paradigm change. However, and this is where relativism might creep in, Kuhn does claim that in addition to these objective criteria, a choice between paradigms 'depends on a mixture of objective and subjective factors' (p. 325). This may just be what leads to accusations of relativism in Kuhn's work, but relativism need not follow as long as neutrality, even if localized, can be had between competing standards of evaluation. As long as philosophers of science do not deny the possibility of neutrality among paradigm (or worldview) choices, relativism need not follow. If neutrality is denied, the view falls suspect to the general self-refuting arguments raised against epistemological relativism in Chapter 2.

RELATIVISM AND POLITICS: THE CASE OF ALASDAIR MACINTYRE

The ironical aspect of the relativist position is that those who take it are also the very ones who champion the 'practical' most profusely, little realizing how utterly impractical applied relativism is. With benevolent and impartial indifference for all and approval for none, you can say that every protagonist of discordant views is right, but you cannot govern a nation that way, unless you want disorder, anarchy, and chaos (Williamson 1947, p. 55).

One way of thinking about relativism in politics is to abstract one's conception of 'the political' from particular policy debates (e.g. should the United States be at war in Iraq? or should we increase federal funding for education?) and to consider the most fundamental questions on the nature of political justice, of the good life that might obtain not only just for individual human beings, but also for human beings living together in community. One contemporary philosopher who presents a very thoughtful account of political philosophy in this sense is Alasdair MacIntyre, especially in his book, *Whose Justice? Which Rationality?* MacIntyre's reflections in that book as well as his other major writings offer some important lessons on the relationships between relativism in other areas of philosophy (especially epistemological relativism) and political life. From his early works in the history of ethics and political philosophy up through today, MacIntyre presents an account of what political life, the good life, the moral life should be. This account of the good life in politics is accompanied by an account of what is true, an epistemology.

The purpose of this section is to show how one's views in one area of philosophy, if they are relativistic, can show up in other areas of philosophy or in areas of inquiry that may lie outside of philosophy proper. The section will focus on the relationship between MacIntyre's account of political ethics and his epistemology. I will argue that while I believe that MacIntyre's advocacy of an Aristotelian/Thomistic account of the political ethics is praiseworthy, I believe that it cannot be reasonably maintained, given MacIntyre's epistemology. Because MacIntyre's epistemology has elements that tend toward epistemic relativism, I believe that this militates against that which is true in MacIntyre's political ethics.

There are three features of good political life that are consistent with MacIntyre's political views: Aristotelian, Thomism and Utopianism. First is the Aristotelian conception of virtue in the individual and virtue in the *polis*, which comes to us by way of the *Nichomachean Ethics*. 'Human good turns out to be activity of soul in conformity with excellence . . . in a complete life' (Aristotle 1995, 1098a15). Part of that complete life will involve external goods, including political human relationships.

This leads to the second element of MacIntyre's political ethics: Thomism. Adding what is known by faith to Aristotle's claims about the good life known by natural reason, Thomas Aquinas agrees that this life contains 'imperfect happiness' and requires external goods, but that perfect happiness does not:

> For man needs in this life, the necessaries of the body, both for the operation of contemplative virtue, and for the operation of active virtue . . . On the other hand, such goods as these are nowise necessary for perfect Happiness, which consists in seeing God . . . [which] will be either in the soul separated from the body, or in the soul united to the body then no longer animal but spiritual. Consequently these external goods are nowise necessary for that Happiness, since they are ordained to the animal life (Aquinas 2006, I-II, Q. 4, Art. 7).

So, for Aquinas, external goods are not necessary for perfect happiness, which is found in the beatific vision.

Third, there is a kind of utopianism present in MacIntyre's works, which he couches at the end of *After Virtue* as a longing for a new St Benedict. The Benedictine Rule contains within it a kind of communal living. Such communalism is surely *possible*, and in one literary reference takes the following form. A vision of such a utopian communal economy is presented in George MacDonald's 'A Shop in Heaven' which is an account of a dream had by one of the character's in MacDonald's novel *Thomas Wingfold: Curate*.

One of MacDonald's characters relates a dream in which he was led by a heavenly guide into a marketplace of shops in heaven which he describes as a place where in the economic exchanges of one to another:

a man there could perfectly read the countenance of every neighbour . . . There was no seeking there, but a strength of giving, a business-like earnestness to supply lack, enlivened by no haste, and dulled by no weariness, brightened ever by the reflected content of those who found their wants supplied, pleasure to see how everyone knew what his desire was, making his choice readily and with decision . . . [which] came not of individual knowledge, but of universal faith and all-embracing love (MacDonald 1996, p. 298).

The dreamer questioned how is it possible that these 'happy people do their business and pass from hand to hand not a single coin?' The reason given to him is:

Where greed and ambition and self-love rule, money must be: where there is neither greed nor ambition nor self-love, money is needless . . . Where neither greed nor ambition nor selfishness reigneth . . . there need and desire have free scope, for they work no evil . . . [I]t is never advantage to himself that moveth a man in this kingdom to undertake this or that. The thing that alone advantageth a man here is the thing which he doth without thought unto that advantage . . . so that when one prayeth, 'Give me, friend, of thy loaves,' a man may answer, 'Take of them, friend, as many as thou needest' – is that, I say, an incentive to diligence less potent than the desire to hoard or to excel? Is it not to share the bliss of God who hoardeth nothing, but ever giveth liberally? The joy of a man here is to enable another to lay hold

RELATIVISM: A GUIDE FOR THE PERPLEXED

upon that which is of his own kind and be glad and grow thereby (p. 302).

The Thomistic beatific vision enables one to be filled with an all-embracing love of God through direct unmediated awareness of the Divine.[8] Although not necessary for complete happiness according to Thomas, external goods of the kind described by MacDonald could be present in a utopian conception of a 'political heaven' as aspects of human life that were a part and parcel of human nature. This type of 'utopian heavenly political economy' may well fit the utopian *telos* embodied in the Aristotelian/Thomistic tradition with which MacIntyre sympathizes.

The question then arises of the possibility of our knowledge of this type of utopia. As an item of knowledge, we must turn now to the four main features of Alisdair MacIntyre's epistemology. They are as follows:

  i. Having knowledge and being rational are dependent on certain perspectival aspects of one 'tradition' or another.[9]
  ii. There is no neutral, i.e. supra or a-traditional way to evaluate competing knowledge or rationality claims.[10]
  iii. There can be rational defeat of one tradition by another.[11]
  iv. An Aristotelian/Thomistic tradition is superior to other traditions.[12]

MacIntyre claims that given his commitment to iii. and iv., i. and ii. do not lead to relativism. The accounts given throughout MacIntyre's works on how traditions defeat one another by demonstrating their problem-solving ability *vis-à-vis* the lights of the other tradition, show relativism simply doesn't follow.[13]

However, it seems that there may be an inconsistency in maintaining ii. and iii. It is inconsistent to maintain that there is no neutral account of rationality and to give a normative account of how traditions defeat one another. If there is no tradition-neutral account of rationality, then there can be no tradition-neutral account of how traditions can rationally defeat one another. Although it is an empirical fact that traditions do in fact interact, an account of the nature of such interactions that is transcendent must, according to MacIntyre, be a description that is only justified within some particular tradition. If rationality is relative, then *everything* about rationality, including principles by which one tradition rationally defeats another, is also relative.[14] MacIntyre is telling us the real condition of human inquiry in a non-tradition-bound sense. Feature iii. presupposes a real non-tradition-bound way of telling us the real condition of human inquiry, but this is precisely what feature ii. denies.

One might claim that while iii. itself is only true from within the tradition in which it is made, nevertheless it can be shown to apply to other traditions just in case one tradition defeats another in the way outlined above. However, this presupposes that MacIntyre's own account of the truth of iii. is correct. If someone from a tradition different from MacIntyre's who maintains not-iii. is confronted with MacIntyre's claim that iii., then how is one to adjudicate between them? According to ii., there can be no appeal to some standard that is neutral between both traditions. Item iii. seems to be functioning as something that is neutral between traditions, but according to ii., there is no such thing. Thus, it appears inconsistent to maintain ii. and iii.

While MacIntyre's works show excellent examples of the interaction and conflicts between and within traditions, there is a real difficulty in offering any extra-traditional justification of the correctness of his account of such confrontation and interaction. As Scott Smith writes, MacIntyre 'is intent on giving us not just a statement of how things are for his way of life . . . but rather a full-blown attempt to persuade others that his is how they *ought* to see the world, too' (Smith 2003, p. 202). Thus, there is a difficulty of providing a consistent non-relative account of how rationality should operate.

Returning now to the application of MacIntyre's epistemology applied to our knowledge of a politically utopian *summum bonum* (USB), i.–iv. cannot reasonably establish the kind of USB that MacIntyre might envision (or any other concept of a USB for that matter).[15] For our purposes here with respect to the discussion of the greatest good, i. above entails i.*:

i.* With respect to what the ultimate good for human life is, the utopian *summum bonum* (USB), a belief *p* about USB can only be made within some tradition (whether religious or otherwise) T, where T provides standards of evaluation such that *p* is judged to be the USB only within the constraints of the standards of epistemic justification within T.

Feature ii. entails ii.*:

> ii.* Given a different tradition T* where USB in T is rejected and USB* is accepted, there is no neutral way to determine which standards of justification to use to determine whether one should accept USB or USB*.

Features iii. and iv. together entail:

> iii.*–iv.* The Aristotelian/Thomistic tradition-bound concept of the USB can (will?) defeat all other present (future?, logically possible?) concepts of the USB.

It appears that i.*–iv.* taken together as a philosophical view may still fall prey to a simple *reductio* argument against relativism. Suppose we label i.*–iv.* as a belief p. It would follow that:

1. If p is itself a position that is reasonable to believe, then the advocate of p must have good reasons for holding to it.
2. If there are good reasons for holding to p, then those good reasons are neutral (by definition of 'good reason').
3. According to p itself, it is not the case that those good reasons are neutral.
4. Therefore, according to the advocate of p, there are not good reasons for holding to p.
5. Thus, there are not good reasons for holding to p.

Further, p is a belief that is found within a belief system (B_1) held by the advocate of p which contains internal to it its own standards of justification s_1-s_n. But, it is possible that on some other belief system (B_2) with standards of justification of s_{1*}-s_{n*}, p is not justified. p might be justified within B_1 but not be justified within B_2. Further, the advocate of p on her own grounds must add that there is no neutral way to adjudicate between B_1 and B_2 in order to establish p or not-p. But this implies that there are no good reasons to accept p. Thus, an advocacy of i.*–iv.* fails. Therefore, no rational establishment of USB can be made, if i.*–iv.* are maintained.

I believe that given i.–iv. entails a problematic form of epistemic relativism it cannot be reasonably applied to a theory of politics. If one wants to have a conception of the good political life, then the thing to do is just to drop feature ii. of one's epistemology. This seems to cause all of the relativistic worries that accompany

MacIntyre's account of knowledge in its application to the USB. There are several possible things that dropping ii. might entail.

First, dropping ii. could lead to a return to the strong rationalistic Cartesian project of searching for an ultimate criterion for all knowledge, the type of which Descartes sought in clarity and distinctness. While the search for one ultimate criterion of clarity and distinctness has proved a failure, what has managed to survive from this Cartesian project is a portion of that search that is still with us today: the denial of the possibility of allowing our minds to be connected to the world in a comprehensive fashion in which the ontological reality and thus the epistemic reality of the so called 'secondary qualities' is rejected. This failure is found in Galileo's tickled statues, Descartes' smelly wax, Locke's hot fire, Berkeley's warm water, and up through the Kantian notion that we can never get to things as they are in themselves. There is in modern philosophy a strong denial of the possibility of allowing our minds to connect rightly with the world. There is a general disappearance of the acceptance of the reality of the so-called 'secondary qualities'. This denial leads Berkeley in his own way and Kant in his to a complete denial of both the 'secondary' and 'primary' qualities being possible objects of knowledge as they are in themselves. This unhappy road, it seems to me, moves from the denial of simple common phenomenal experiences like colours or felt qualities and moves directly and irrecoverably into a denial of the objective reality of moral qualities (e.g Hume). This loss I believe makes impossible an objectivity of knowledge of either a temporal or eternal political utopia.

Giving up ii. could entail moving to a stronger rejection of knowledge as a possibility altogether, as presented by Richard Rorty who is sympathetic with feature ii. of MacIntyre's epistemology:

> For unless a knowledge of the function of the human species takes us beyond MacIntyre's Socratic claims that 'the good life for man is the life spent in seeking for the good life for man' (MacIntyre AV, p. 204), the idea of one narrative being more 'objective and authoritative' than another, as opposed to being more detailed and inclusive, goes by the board (Rorty 1991, p. 161, footnote 30).

Following Rorty, to give up ii. as something we *know* could be consistent with a radical rejection of the possibility of knowledge as such in preference for something else altogether: ' "The nature of truth" is an unprofitable topic . . . But this claim about relative profitability, in turn, is just the recommendation that we in fact *say* little about these topics, and see how we get on' (Rorty 1989, p. 8). This rejection of ii. leads more into a relativistic morass than accepting it, and thus should be rejected as MacIntyre himself recognizes, when he states,

> At perhaps its most fundamental level I can state the disagreement between Rorty and myself in the following way. His dismissal of 'objective' or 'rational' standards emerges from the writing of genealogical history . . . but at once the question arises of whether he has written a history that is in fact true; and to investigate that question, I should want to argue, is to discover that the practice of writing true history requires implicit or explicit references to standards of objectivity and rationality of just the kind that the initial genealogical history was designed to discredit (MacIntyre 1982, p. 109).[16]

Since a return to Cartesian hopes for single criterion coupled with a rejection of the possibility of the mind's connection with what is real, and a rejection of the possibility of knowledge as such are non-starters, there are other ways to make progress towards our knowledge and acquisition of a political utopian *summum bonum*. We need to reject ii. in favour of an epistemology in which there is neutrality between any competing epistemic traditions. Such an account would require three things: 1. a strong view of human essentialism about personhood using the resources of Aristotelian/Thomistic essentialist biology; 2. a return to the objectivity of knowledge; 3. a return to the objectivity of value.

First, a rejection of the second feature of MacIntyre's epistemology can be plausibly accomplished just in case there is an essential human nature shared by all rational beings. If human beings share an essential human nature, rational-animality or the *imago dei*, this may serve as a neutral *sameness* by means of which disputes in morality or politics or even about knowledge itself can be adjudicated. A full-blown account of an Aristotelian/Thomistic view of personhood is well beyond the scope of this work, but the way forward on such an account is solvable in principle simply by comparing the explanatory power of materialist/physicalist accounts of human nature with those of an Aristotelian/Thomistic one on such areas as the unity of the self at a time and across time and with respect to freedom of the will. In the first area of the unity of the self, for example, an Aristotelian account of the reality of teleology in natural organisms has great explanatory power in making sense of the available data that explains the role and function of genetic information as well as the law-like processes apparent in organic growth.[17] A properly developed Aristotelian account of the soul provides a necessary component for the possibility of the univocity of knowledge across human enquirers, even if those enquirers are epistemically tradition dependent.

Second, a rejection of feature ii. can be safely accomplished just in case an account of the objectivity of knowledge can be defended along both epistemic and ontologically realistic lines. Such an account would maintain that knowledge is an act or disposition of representing things as they are on the appropriate basis of thought and experience.[18]

Such an account has three features. 1) Knowledge is an act of disposition of representing things. This first component requires a realistic, non-causal account of perception such that the mind is directly, immediately (say goodbye to the modern notions of ideas) aware of the objects it is perceiving. 2) Knowledge represents *things as they are*. This account of knowledge requires a strong correspondence theory of truth set up along metaphysically realistic lines, which pays careful attention to the real phenomenology of truth in our ordinary experience.[19] If there is to be any account of a political utopian *summum bonum*, this account must be able to rest upon an adequate theory of truth such that the account given can be seen to be true by any serious enquirer. We do this all the time in common-sense activities. I tell you where the bookstore is; you represent where the bookstore is in your mind; you move throughout the world to see if your idea matches reality; you *see* that your idea of where the bookstore is matches the reality you experience as you stand in front of the bookstore. If we can do this with bookstores, it does not seem impossible to do it with other places we long for like a political utopian *summum bonum*. 3) Representing things as they are, of course, must be done on the 'appropriate basis' of thought and experience. It is this level of what is often called epistemic 'justification' that seems rather vague in the notion of knowledge advocated here. Perhaps this is not such a bad thing. The appropriateness of the standards of justification may simply be pegged to the area of enquiry. I don't go about looking for my soul in exactly the same way I look for my sole. Justification might still be foundational, but it is dependent on the subject matter in question. This type of account of the objectivity of knowledge, if plausible, will go a long way in replacing feature ii. of MacIntyre's epistemology.

This brings us to the third requirement for an epistemology that rejects MacIntyre's feature ii, which allows us to maintain a clear vision for the utopian *summum bonum*. The objectivity of value is largely lost to our culture today. Whatever one's opinion of Alan Bloom's *Closing of the American Mind*, traditionalist and progressive professors alike can, through reflection of their most recent experience teaching an introductory philosophy course, readily agree with Bloom that one thing that is true about undergraduates is that they are nearly without exception ethical (if not total philosophical) relativists.[20] Without an account of the objectivity of value, which is dependent on an objective epistemology sketched above, no progress is possible for knowledge of the political utopian *summum bonum* whatsoever. However, as Rene De Visme Williamson writes,

> The tricky thing about the objectivity of value is that it cannot be proved. It might be conceded that if mortal man is the ultimate source of all truth and is, as Protagoras [the first relativist] taught, the measure of all things, this is the best answer [that politics should be solely based on consent rather than on objective moral truths] that one could give. Nevertheless, it is not nearly good enough. In the first place, it is not true that there are no values above and beyond man. It is not a valid argument against the existence of absolute values to assert that we cannot prove that they exist to someone who doubts it or to cite numerous cases in which men have been mistaken in identifying and applying them. There are a great many things in this world which are true and yet undemonstrable. It is the sight of the onlooker which is at fault and not the visibility of the object (Williamson 1947, p. 157).

The real foundation for human reasoning itself, our knowledge of what is real, good, true, beautiful, and our knowledge of any political *summum bonum*, requires that there be a real objective moral order that we can know and appropriate into our moral and social lives.

In his exposition of the philosophical points of *Veritatis Splendor*, MacIntyre himself specifies the three points made here: the need for an essentialist account of human nature, the explication of the objectivity of knowledge and a commitment to the objectivity of value. MacIntyre writes,

> But insofar as the conception of human nature which we arrive at is indeed that of human nature as structured by the natural law,[21] we will have succeeded in transcending what is peculiar to our own or any other culture. It will have become a conception of that which 'is itself a measure of culture', of that in human beings which shows that they are 'not exhaustively defined' by their culture and are not its prisoner. So once again a connection between truth and freedom[22] appears. Just as we are not to be explained as wholly determined by our physical and biological make-up, so we are not merely products of our cultural environment, but actual or potential creative shapers of it, precisely insofar as we can evaluate its perspectives in terms which are non-perspectival,[23] the terms of truth[24] (MacIntyre 1994, p. 188).

MacIntyre here has pinpointed the philosophical commitments required to eliminate feature ii. of his own epistemology. Those of us who have learned a great deal from MacIntyre's work will continue to explore his philosophy in this direction with him in order to avoid the logical and practical problems associated with relativism as applied to political theories.

RELATIVISM AND RELIGION: THE CASES OF BLASPHEMY AND HERESY

'Relativism has thus become the central problem for the faith at the present time' (Cardinal Joseph Ratzinger/Pope Benedict XVI).[25]

Relativism is a problem for religious belief for two reasons. First, relativism poses a direct challenge to the objectivity of religious beliefs. If relativism were true, then the solutions to the problems facing the human condition (e.g. our need for love, the existence of evil, and the reality of death) which are presented by various religious traditions won't be real solutions for all people at all times. They will simply be relative solutions that may *work for* (whatever that means) members of that particular faith community. Second, relativism, if true, reduces religious knowledge claims to mere belief, and this runs contrary to what many (especially conservative) religious traditions actually claim. For example, Orthodox Jews really believe that God gave the Law (e.g. the Ten Commandments) directly to Moses; Christians believe (e.g. the Nicene Creed) that Jesus was raised from the dead; Muslims believe that the Quran is Allah's final revelation to mankind. If relativism is right, then all of these beliefs, many of which are inconsistent with one another, are simply beliefs, but not knowledge. However, adherents to these religious traditions don't think that these are mere beliefs; they take them to be items of knowledge. So, relativism if true undermines the very objectivity of religion that so many religious people take to be the case, especially with respect to their specific religious beliefs.

One way of thinking about religious relativism is to think about the concepts of blasphemy and heresy. Heresy is understood to be an act committed by subject S in the case where S, a member of a religious (or other) belief system R, believes h where h is a chosen rejection of a widely accepted belief p within and central to R, and blasphemy is committed by S in the case where S believes p where p contains an irreverent or profane rejection of a widely accepted belief q within a religious (or other) belief system.[26] With respect to relativism, there is a distinction between two ways in which heresy and blasphemy are relative to religious traditions: (1) a trivial way and (2) a substantial way. On the trivial way, heresy and blasphemy are relative to a religion in that for a claim even to be considered as heretical or blasphemous it must be made within a particular religion, where the orthodox or pious beliefs are centrally important to the religion. For example, the claim p: 'Jesus was not crucified' is only heretical within the Christian religion, but not heretical within, say, Athena worship, since p is not central to Athena worship, or within Islam since p is believed to be true within Islam, and so cannot be heretical. However, on the substantial (and I think problematic) way in which heresy and blasphemy are relative to religious traditions, not only is a belief p trivially relative, but p is thought to be true or justified only within that particular religion, such that the truth of p is generated or made by the standards of the religion in which it is made.

The substantial relativistic rejection of blasphemy/heresy claims that the reality of the concepts of blasphemy and heresy are merely relative to the religious system in which they are being used. There may be putative blasphemers or heretics, but there are no real blasphemers, because to really blaspheme or to err in one's religious belief is really impossible. This is due to the fact that the opposites of blasphemy and heresy, i.e. reverence and orthodoxy, contain within them beliefs the truths of which are simply relative to the religious traditions from within which they are made.

The substantial relativist account of blasphemy might take the following two-part approach:[27]

1. A putatively blasphemous or heretical belief p is blasphemous or heretical only within some religious (or other) belief system R, where R provides standards of evaluation such that p is judged to be heretical or blasphemous only within the constraints of the standards of epistemic justification within R.
2. Given a different religious (or other) belief system R* (where the blasphemous or heretical belief within R is established as pious or orthodox or both), there is no neutral way to determine which standards of justification to use to determine the orthodoxy or piety of p.

So, for example, the relativist might make use of the following:
On the one hand, an Orthodox Christian claims to have established p,

p: Jesus was divine in nature and not created by God,

by means of the following standards of evaluation S_1 found only within Christianity (R_1),

S_1: Consistency with the accounts of the New Testament and Church Tradition.

For the Orthodox Christian, S_1 is a legitimate standard found only within the constraints of R_1 making p an orthodox belief within R_1 and $\sim p$ a heretical belief within R_1.
On the other hand, an Arian Christian claims to have established q,

q: Jesus was not divine in nature and was created by God,[28]

by means of the following standard of evaluation S_2 found only within Arianism (R_2),

S_2: Consistency with philosophical assumptions of Greek philosophy.

For the Arian, S_2 is a legitimate standard found only within the constraints of R_2, making q an orthodox belief within R_2 and $\sim q$ a heretical belief within R_2.

The relativist will further add that given a dispute between S_1 found within R_1 and S_2 found within R_2, there is no neutral way to adjudicate between these two standards of evaluation that are relative to the religions in which they occur. Thus, one person's putative orthodoxy is another person's putative heresy. Thus, the concepts of orthodoxy/heresy and blasphemy/reverence are concepts which are not real at all in the sense that they point to something that is independent of the particular justification standards found within a particular religious tradition. These concepts are merely relative concepts. There is no real heresy (or orthodoxy), only 'heresy within' or 'heresy for' particular groups within a religious tradition. There is no real blasphemy (or reverence), only 'blasphemy within' or 'blasphemy for' a particular religious person in a religious tradition. This completes the relativistic denial of the existence of blasphemy or heresy.

This relativistic denial of the possibility of blasphemy or heresy, however, is mistaken, because it rests on a faulty relativistic epistemology. Relativism about blasphemy or heresy functions as a broader instance of a type of self-defeating epistemological relativism that can be shown to be faulty by considering a fairly straightforward *reductio* argument, which we also applied to political relativism in the previous section.

1. If the relativistic account of the relativism of blasphemy and heresy is itself a position that is reasonable to believe, then the relativist must have good reasons for holding to it.
2. If there are good reasons for holding to the relativist's position, then those good reasons are neutral (by definition of 'good reason').
3. According to the relativist, it is not the case that those good reasons are neutral.
4. Therefore, according to the relativist, there are not good reasons for holding to the relativist's own position.
5. Thus, there are not good reasons for holding to the relativist's own position.

Further, the relativistic account of blasphemy or heresy (RHB) is a belief that is found within a belief system (B_1) held by the relativist which contains internal to it its own standards of justification s_1-s_n. But, it is possible that on some other belief system (B_2) with standards of justification of s_{j*}-s_{n*}, RHB is not justified. RHB might be justified within B_1 but not be justified within B_2. Further, the relativist on her own grounds must add that there is no neutral way to adjudicate between B_1 and B_2 in order to establish RHB or ~RHB. But this implies that there are no good reasons to accept RHB. Thus, the relativistic denial of the possibility of real blasphemy and real heresy fails.

It is not my intention to argue for or against the orthodoxy or piety of any particular religious belief (i.e. to point out which beliefs are heretical or blasphemous). It is simply to show that contra a relativist's denial, heresy and blasphemy are real possibilities, that it could turn out that there are religious beliefs which are blasphemous (or pious) and heretical (or orthodox). The real possibility of these concepts comes from a consideration of the reasons that (in our case) religious people have for holding the beliefs that they hold. For example, in our case above, an Orthodox Christian might have reasons for holding to her standards of justification. Such reasons might include the reliability of certain other historical data presented in the New Testament (e.g. archaeological confirmations of Gospel claims). Similarly, an Orthodox Muslim might have reasons for holding to her standards of justification. For example, the Quran itself might be considered as a book the properties of which cannot be explained other than through an appeal to a divine miracle. These are non-arbitrary reasons, and may turn out to be really good reasons for holding to the standards of justification that these religious believers have. Neither the Christian nor the Muslim must necessarily be committed to the possibility of these particular standards of justification as being the standards that solve all of the disputes about whose beliefs are heretical or blasphemous and whose are not. However, they are (in virtue of having non-arbitrary reasons for their standards of justification) committed to the possibility of a kind of 'local neutrality' that provides the epistemic space for them possibly to adjudicate their dispute. Such adjudication would focus on the epistemic or evidentiary goodness of the reasons that each disputant has for their standards of epistemic justification. This implies that religious orthodox and pious knowledge is a real possibility. This may also imply a need for free enquiry between religious traditions in order that the opposing reasons for the justification standards within each tradition can be rationally (as opposed to non-rationally, e.g. by force) adjudicated.[29]

TOWARDS NEUTRALITY OF COMPETING STANDARDS OF EVALUATION[30]

Since philosophical beliefs (whether they be general in the areas of ontology, epistemology or axiology, or specific in the areas of science, religion or politics) are established by often disparate and competing standards, we may not have a globally neutral way to determine which standards we should accept, once and for all, for all epistemic disputes, but this does not entail relativism. To the contrary, it entails non-relativism. Given a philosophical dispute, it is possible for there to be a neutral meta-standard that can adjudicate between two competing standards of evaluation. Such a standard must be at least non-arbitrary according to both disputants, and it must not beg the question against either standard of evaluation. In addition, this locally neutral standard must be such that if its conditions are met, one of the standards in dispute will be fairly judged to fare worse than, or be inferior to, the other standard.

This can be demonstrated by a general logical point regarding the nature or meaning of disputes between competing standards of epistemic evaluation. The fact of a dispute implies that local neutrality is a real possibility. Given a dispute between standards of epistemic evaluation, necessarily it is possible for there to be a locally neutral standard between them.

It is possible to ask the person trying to establish some proposition *why* they accept the standards they do, rather than some other standards. Either they were chosen arbitrarily, or they were chosen for some *reason*. If the standards one uses were chosen arbitrarily, then the person who holds to those standards can make no claim that those standards are better than any other standards. If one selects one's standards of evaluation for *no reason*, then one's defence of why one uses those standards cannot be a rational defence, since arbitrary reasons for choosing certain standards over other standards are not good reasons for choosing the standards one uses.

Let us say quite generally that to select non-arbitrarily one set of standards of evaluation instead of another as the standards by means of which one establishes a proposition p, is necessarily to maintain that those standards better establish p (or establish p with fewer problems) than any other standards. The non-question-begging reasons that one has for accepting one's standards used to establish p will have something to them which other standards of evaluation lack. For example, if the standard of evaluation is explanatory power, then to maintain that explanatory power establishes p is to maintain that there are good reasons to choose this standard over and above others, and that with respect to this standard, p is justified.

For any given epistemic dispute, if one of the sides in the debate thinks that they have non-question-begging good reasons for the standards that they use, then that side is committed to the possibility of local neutrality. It is one's acceptance of one's standards as non-arbitrary and non-question-begging that commits one to the possibility of local neutrality. The possibility of local neutrality is found in each side's claim that their own reasons for accepting the standards that they use are non-question-begging good reasons. Thus, given a dispute concerning standards of evaluation, if each side maintains that the reasons that they have for the standards that establish the claim in question are non-question-begging, non-arbitrary, good reasons, then each side is claiming to have good reasons for their standards that should be found persuasive by their rational opponents. This implies that each side will necessarily be committed to the possibility of some locally neutral way of determining which standards of evaluation should be used to solve the dispute.

This logical argument for the possibility of local neutrality centres on the nature or meaning of what it is to *have* standards of epistemic evaluation that one takes to be backed by non-arbitrary good reasons. From the fact that a person has standards of epistemic evaluation, if one holds those standards for what one takes to be good reasons, it logically follows that one regards local neutrality as a real possibility. Whatever the standards of epistemic evaluation one has, if one has those standards, it follows that one may have those standards for reasons that one takes to be good, non-arbitrary, non-question-begging reasons. If one takes her standards of epistemic evaluation to be had for good, non-arbitrary, non-question-begging reasons, then one is committed to the possibility of local neutrality.

Thus, having standards that one takes to be non-arbitrary entails the possibility of local neutrality. This means that if a relativist accepts the standards conjunct of the definition of relativism, the relativist must also accept that local neutrality is a real possibility. If local neutrality is a real possibility, then the relativist cannot hold the second conjunct (i.e. that there is no neutrality between competing standards) in the definition of relativism consistently. Thus, relativism cannot get off the ground, once one acknowledges that one has standards of epistemic evaluation, which one takes oneself to hold for non-arbitrary, non-question-begging, good reasons.

If the relativist were to claim that people have epistemic standards, but they have them for *no reason* at all, the relativist's position would be rather unconvincing and would amount to a mere statement of belief. The relativist would have to be consistent and state that the claim that people have epistemic standards for no reason at all is something that the relativist holds for *no reason at all*, but this does not make the relativist's case very persuasive.

To repeat the argument, we begin by recognizing that for any standard of epistemic evaluation there will be reasons that a person has for having those standards. From the fact that a person has standards of epistemic evaluation, there are only two possible options for *why* a person has those standards. They either maintain those standards for arbitrary reasons, or they maintain them for non-arbitrary reasons.

However, if the reasons are arbitrary, then they are irrational and thus not *good* reasons. The idea of *arbitrary* reasons that are *good* reasons (i.e. epistemically forceful reasons) is contradictory; it is as absurd as a silent noise. In fact, it would be self-defeating to maintain the claim that all one's reasons for maintaining epistemic standards are arbitrary, since the reasons for maintaining this proposition itself will be purely arbitrary, and thus there will be no more reason for accepting this proposition than its negation. Thus, reasons cannot be held arbitrarily and still be counted as good reasons by the person who holds them. Thus, the reasons for maintaining standards of epistemic evaluation must be thought to be non-arbitrary. If they are thought to be non-arbitrary, then one is committed to the possibility of local neutrality.

Thomas Nagel succinctly points out this problem in his little book *The Last Word*. Nagel states, 'The serious attempt to identify what is subjective and communal in one's outlook leads inevitably to the objective and universal' (Nagel 1997, p. 16). Nagel recognizes that we may not need Cartesian certainty about the standards of epistemic evaluation (similar to the recognition that we may not have global standards), and recognizes that we can have a kind of

objectivity to reasons for our local standards of epistemic evaluation. In recognizing the possibility of local neutrality, one can on
Nagel's view offer reasons for the standards one has. Nagel points
out that he wants to give the last word 'to the justifications [i.e.
reasons for our epistemic standards] themselves, including some
that are involved or implicated in that recognition, which is subor-
dinate to them' (p. 34). This is a nice application of the distinction
between what I'm here calling local and global neutrality.

We began with the relativistic claim that given a conflict between
differing standards of evaluation there is no neutral way to choose
which standard of evaluation one should use. It has been shown,
however, that necessarily, given a conflict between differing standards of evaluation, if one takes her standards of evaluation to be
supported by non-arbitrary, non-question-begging good reasons,
then one is committed to the possibility of establishing a locally
neutral way to adjudicate between standards of evaluation. One's
commitment to the possibility of establishing a neutral standard
centres on the fact that there is a real dispute between competing
standards, standards that the disputants take to be grounded in non-
question-begging reasons for holding to those standards. Thus, contrary to the relativist, it is possible for there to be neutral ways to
settle conflicts between competing standards of epistemic evaluation.

CONCLUSION

This text has covered rather quickly a whole range of issues regarding relativistic thought and its application to various areas of
enquiry both inside and outside the discipline of philosophy. While
this little guide for the perplexed has no sympathy for the self-
defeating and logically problematic forms of relativism, it must be
remembered that some relativistic ideas may have something to
teach us. Epistemological relativism teaches us that what we often
may be dogmatic in believing may turn out to be false; ontological
relativism may teach us that what we believe to be the totality of
reality, may be only a portion; ethical relativism may help to remind
us that the norms of our own culture may not be entirely morally
good. While these insights must be kept in mind, philosophers
and others in the academy who care about the life of the mind
must always recognize the difficulties that accompany relativism. We

do this in order to attain what Moses Maimonides (author of the original *Guide for the Perplexed*) calls the 'true perfection' of human life: 'the possession of the highest, intellectual faculties; the possession of such notions which lead to true metaphysical opinions . . .' (Maimonides 1995, Ch. LIV).

NOTES

1. A DEFINITION AND BRIEF HISTORY OF RELATIVISM

1 See also Buss 2004.
2 Portions of this chapter are adapted from Mosteller 2006a. For another excellent introduction to definitions of relativism see Phillips 2007, chapter 1.
3 For a more comprehensive treatment of the history of relativism see Baghramian 2004, pp. 21–36. Baghramian's treatment of the history of relativism from antiquity to the 21st century is excellent, and deserves careful study.
4 The problem is that it is self-defeating.
5 If you find Nietzsche perplexing, see *Nietzsche: A Guide for the Perplexed* (Hill 2007).
6 Schiller develops his philosophy in the tradition of the American pragmatism of Peirce, James, Dewey and Mead, although one may question whether Schiller's relativism is the logical extension of this line of pragmatic philosophers.
7 For a polemical account of the use of the charge of relativism in the so-called 'culture wars', see DiLeanardo 1996.

2. EPISTEMOLOGICAL RELATIVISM

1 This chapter is adapted directly from a longer treatment of epistemic relativism in Mosteller 2006a, chapters 2 and 3.
2 For a recent example of this see Stephen Hales' *Relativism and the Foundations of Philosophy* (Hales 2006).
3 Other contemporary definitions of relativism recognize this dual aspect of relativism: the relevance of 'standards' and the absence of epistemic 'neutrality'. See Harré and Krausz 1996, p. 75; Bayley 1992, p. 2; Gifford 1983, p. x.
4 While Siegel does not use the global/local terminology, it captures Siegel's points.

5 For a concise treatment of the connection between self-defeating relativism and scepticism, see Luper 2004.

6 See also Siegel 1987, pp. 24–5 for additional criticism of Jordan's position.

7 For additional formulations of the self-defeating difficulties with relativism, see Lockie 2003.

8 We might call this 'group solipsism' or 'sol-*us*-ism'.

9 For the solipsist, the existence of all things is dependent on the mental states of the solipsist, but for the epistemological relativist, the *truth* about all things, including other minds, is dependent on the mental states of the relativist. Thus, ER is like solipsism, but in a weaker sense that it does not have a metaphysical commitment in which the existence of other things is dependent on the relativist's mind.

10 Burnyeat is here considering Protagorean relativism, which is somewhat different from Putnam's first-person relativism; the similarity between them is that there is some kind of isolation that occurs when relativism in either form is maintained.

11 Putnam states, 'Truth, in the only sense in which we have a vital and working notion of it, is rational acceptability (or, rather, rational acceptability under sufficiently good epistemic conditions; and which conditions are epistemically better or worse is relative to the type of discourse in just the way rational acceptability itself is)' (Putnam 1981, p. 231).

12 Three very different contemporary epistemologists are in agreement that the notion of justification includes an element of truth indicativeness. See Haack 1993, pp. 81–9, for a 'foundherentist' understanding of justification involving evidence for a belief's being true, Goldman 1986, p. 3, and Bonjour 1985, p. 8.

13 Putnam gives the following example:

To spell this out, suppose R.R., a cultural relativist, says:
When Karl says 'Schnee ist weiss', what Karl means (whether he knows it or not) is that snow is white *as determined* by the norms of Karl's culture (which we now take to be German culture).
Now the sentence 'Snow is white is determined by the norms of German culture' is itself one that R.R. has to *use*, not just mention, to say what Karl says. On his own account, what R.R. means by *this* sentence is:
'Snow is white as determined by the norms of German culture' is true by the norms of R.R.'s culture (which we take to be American culture).
Substituting this back into the first displayed utterance (and changing to indirect quotation) yields:
When Karl says 'Schnee ist weiss', what he means (whether he knows it or not) is that it is true as determined by the norms of American culture that it is true as determined by the norms of German culture that snow is white.
In general, if R.R. understands *every* utterance *p* that *he* uses as meaning 'it is true by the norms of American culture that *p*', then he must understand his own hermeneutical utterances, the utterances he uses to interpret others, the same way . . . Other cultures become, so to

speak, logical constructions out of the procedures and practices of American culture (Putnam 1981, p. 237) (Putnam's emphasis).

14 When the relativist says that in her culture, the concept of truth is 'xyz', then her claim will be true only in her culture, which is itself problematic as shown in the analysis of the general difficulties with relativism in Chapters 1 and 2, but if the relativist makes the additional claim that the concept of truth in a second person's culture is 'xyz', then the claim that the concept of truth in the second person's culture is 'xyz' will only be true in the relativist's culture.

3. ONTOLOGICAL RELATIVISM

1 I owe my understanding of both of these general responses to ontological relativism to Dallas Willard.

2 I owe this example to my colleague Todd Bates.

3 If you find Kant perplexing, see *Kant: A Guide for the Perplexed* (Seung 2007).

4 See Case 2001, p. 418.

5 This type of example is found throughout Putnam's work (Putnam 1988, chapter 4; 1992, p. 120; 1993, p. 309; 1994, p. 450; 2004, pp. 33–51). I believe it is a central one that must be addressed when evaluating the coherence of Putnam's internal realism. See also Throop and Doran 1991, p. 360, for this same point.

6 In a footnote to his sketch of his previous views on how 'we can have referential access to external things', Putnam states that in his previous work, *The Many Faces of Realism* (Putnam 1987), he 'identified it with the rejection of the traditional realist assumptions of 1) a fixed totality of all objects; 2) a fixed totality of all properties; 3) a sharp line between properties we "discover" in the world and properties we "project onto the world"; 4) a fixed relation of "correspondence" in terms of which truth is supposed to be defined. I rejected those assumptions not as false assumptions, but as ultimately unintelligible assumptions . . . I still regard each and every one of those assumptions as unintelligible' (footnote 41, p. 463).

7 For an excellent introduction and overview of Quinean ontological relativism, see O'Grady 2002.

4. ETHICAL RELATIVISM

1 For a short selection from Benedict's book (as well as other excellent primary source readings) see Moser and Carson 2000.

2 The official metre stick is located in Sèvres, France, at the Bureau International des Poids et Mesures.

3 Philosophers disagree whether there is a 'moral stick' analogous to the metre stick, or if there is one, whether it can be housed anywhere at all!

4 For a similar, but longer, list see Beckwith and Koukl (1998).

5. AESTHETIC RELATIVISM

1 For a slightly more technical discussion along these lines, see Beardsley 1983.
2 One problem here in this quotation is that if Hyman means that reject-ing the 'idea that there is a single model of truth and perfection in the visual arts' is a denial of the possibility of neutrality between competing standards of aesthetic judgements, then it seems to me that his reminder has slipped into a more problematic prescriptivist version of aesthetic relativism, discussed below.
3 See also Young 2001, pp. 116ff, for a similar discussion of relativism in art. Young believes that if art has a cognitive function this may militate against more radical, or as Davey calls them 'dogmatic', positions of aesthetic relativism.
4 If you find Hume perplexing, see *Hume: A Guide for the Perplexed* (Coventry 2007).
5 The notion of the 'form' of an argument could be an aesthetic notion, and not merely a logical one. If so, this could make a formally valid argu-ment beautiful. I owe this suggestion to Todd Bates.
6 Axiology is the study of values generally, which, in my view, consists of both moral goods, i.e. ethics and non-moral goods, i.e. aesthetics.

6. RELATIVISTIC WORLDVIEWS IN SCIENCE, POLITICS AND RELIGION, AND THE POSSIBILITY OF NEUTRALITY

1 This is indirect realism, which is a dominant theme of modernity, from Galileo to Kant.
2 In the modern period this began with the so-called 'secondary qualities', e.g. taste, touch, smell (Galileo, Locke, Descartes), and ended up includ-ing the so-called 'secondary qualities', e.g. extension, solidity, in the scep-ticism of Hume, the Idealism of Berkeley or the Critical Idealism of Kant.
3 It may not be self-defeating if there is knowledge that is had without proof. If nothing is known without proof, nothing could be known by means of proof. Unless some things are known prior to worldview nothing could be known from a worldview, including our knowledge of the nature of worldview.
4 Like Pluto, it could lose its planetary status.
5 The discussion that follows is adapted from Mosteller 2006a.
6 Kuhn points out that through observation and reason unaided by tech-nological and mathematical advances, the ancients were convinced that the earth as a moving planet was an absurd notion (p. 43).
7 See Siegel 1987, chapter 3, for an extensive discussion of Kuhnian rela-tivism. I am simply using this historical example (which Kuhn uses to develop his arguments regarding how scientific progress is related to par-adigm shifts) to show a particular case in which local neutrality might be had. It must be noted that Kuhn downplays the importance of such locally neutral standards in explaining scientists' acceptance of one par-

adigm over another. I am simply using these locally neutral standards raised by Kuhn to show that, contrary to the epistemological relativist, local neutrality can in fact be had.

8 Dante concludes, 'My will and my desire were turned by love, the love that moves the sun and other stars' (Dante 1962, p. 347, canto XXXIII, lines 142–5).

9 See MacIntyre 1971, p. 247; 1984, p. 222; 1988, p. 7.

10 See MacIntyre 1988, pp. 166, 350, 351, 367.

11 See MacIntyre 1984, pp. 276–7; 1988, pp. 166–7, 354.

12 See MacIntyre 1988, pp. 402–3; 1990, p. 2.

13 See Mosteller 2006a, chapter 3, for a longer treatment of relativism in MacIntyre's epistemology, from which this section is adapted.

14 For additional criticisms and discussions of this point see also: Feldman 1986, p. 316; Isaac 1989, p. 667; Lutz 2004, p. 77; Smith 2003, pp. 198–200; Snider 1989, p. 390; Wallace 1989, p. 345; and Weinstein 2003, pp. 88–91.

15 This is the same type of argument that we have been levelling against relativistic ideas throughout this work.

16 This same argument, I claim above, applies to MacIntyre's views as well as Rorty's. See Mosteller 2006a chapter 5, for a lengthy treatment of relativism in the philosophy of Richard Rorty.

17 See Connell 1988 and Gilson 1984.

18 This account of formulating knowledge was presented to me by Dallas Willard.

19 There are several recent works in realistic correspondence theories of truth. Newman 2002; Vision 2004; Fumerton 2002.

20 For a fascinating empirical study of the rise of relativism in contemporary culture see Dawson and Stein 2004.

21 This is a commitment both to the natural law (i.e. the objectivity of value) and to essentialist view of human nature.

22 I.e. what is epistemic and what is ethical.

23 This seems to be a clear rejection of feature ii. of MacIntyre's epistemology.

24 I.e. a commitment to the objectivity of knowledge.

25 See Ratzinger 1996 (an address to the Congregation for the Doctrine of the Faith, Guadalajara, Mexico).

26 Eleanor Stump has argued that heresy requires that the person intentionally rejects a central tenet of the religion in which the heresy is committed (Stump 1999). The definitions I am using here operate on the assumption that one can pick out beliefs that constitute heresy, which, as Alvin Plantinga has pointed out, can be quite difficult (Plantinga 1999).

27 This account of relativism is taken from Siegel 1987, p. 6.

28 This is the Christian heresy of Arianism, from Arius (A.D. 250–336) which is roughly the idea that Jesus was not one nature with God but was created by God.

29 See, 'Why We Need Interreligious Polemics' (Griffiths 1994) for a description of this type of interaction.

30 This section is adapted directly from Mosteller 2006a and 2006b.

WORKS CITED

Aquinas, St Thomas (2006), *Summa Theologica*, Project Gutenberg Online Edition, http://www.gutenberg.org/files/17897/17897.txt.

Aristotle (1995), *The Complete Works of Aristotle*, Princeton, NJ: Princeton University Press.

Baghramian, Maria (2004), *Relativism*, London: Routledge.

Barna Group (2002), 'Americans Are Most Likely to Base Truth on Feelings', http://www.barna.org/FlexPage.aspx?Page=BarnaUpdate&BarnaUpdate ID=106.

Bayley, Eric (1999), 'Suppressed Speeches Fuel Religion-in-Schools Battle', *Los Angeles Times*, 24 June, p. 1, Metro Section.

Bayley, James (1992), *Aspects of Relativism*, Lanham, MD: University Press of America.

Beardsley, Monroe (1983), 'The Refutation of Relativism', *The Journal of Aesthetics and Art Criticism*, Vol. 41, No. 3, pp. 265–70.

Beckwith, Frank and Koukl, Greg (1998), *Relativism: Feet Firmly Planted in Mid-Air*, Grand Rapids, Mich: Baker.

Benedict, Ruth (1934), *Patterns of Cuture*, New York, NY: Houghton Mifflin.

Bloom, Alan (1987), *The Closing of the American Mind*, New York, NY: Simon and Schuster.

Bonjour, Laurence (1985), *The Structure of Empirical Knowledge*, Cambridge, Mass: Harvard University Press.

Boring, Edwin G. (1930), 'A New Ambiguous Figure', *American Journal of Psychology*, 42: 444–5.

Borst, Clive (1994), 'Solipsism', *A Companion to Epistemology*, Oxford: Blackwell.

Burke, Peter (1985), *Vico*, Oxford: Oxford University Press.

Burnyeat, M. F. (1976), 'Protagoras and Self-Refutation in Plato's Theatetus', *The Philosophical Review*, Vol. LXXXV, No. 2, pp. 172–95.

Buss, Dale (2004), 'Christian Teens? Not Very', *Wall Street Journal*, 9 July.

Case, Jennifer (2001), 'The Heart of Putnam's Pluralistic Realism', *Revue Internationale de Philosophie*, No. 218, pp. 123–40.

Connell, Richard (1988), *Substance and Modern Science*, Houston, Tex: Center for Thomistic Studies.

Copleston, Frederick (1993), *A History of Philosophy*, New York, NY: Image Books.

Coventry, Angela (2007), *Hume: A Guide for the Perplexed*, London: Continuum.

Craig, William Lane and Moreland, J. P. (2003), *Philosophical Foundations for a Christian Worldview*, Downers Grove, Ill: InterVarsity Press.

Dante, Alighieri (1962), *The Divine Comedy*, translated by Dorothy Sayers, New York, NY: Basic Books.

Davey, Nicholas (1992), 'Relativism', *A Companion to Aesthetics*, edited by David Cooper, Oxford: Blackwell, p. 358.

Dawson-Tunik, Theo and Stein, Zachary (2004), *The Development of Relativism*, http://www.lectica.info/images/Relativism.pdf.

DiLeonardo, Micaela (1996), 'Patterns of Culture Wars', *The Nation*, 8 April, pp. 25–9.

Feldman, Susan (1986), 'Objectivity, Pluralism, and Relativism', *Southern Journal of Philosophy*, Vol. 24, No. 3, pp. 307–20.

Fumerton, Richard (2002), *Realism and the Correspondence Theory of Truth*, Lanham, MD: Rowman and Littlefield.

Geertz, Clifford (1984), 'Anti-Anti-Relativism', *American Anthropologist*, Vol. 86, No. 2, pp. 263–78.

Gifford, N. L. (1983), *When in Rome: An Introduction to Relativism and Knowledge*, Albany, New York, NY: State University of New York Press.

Gilson, Etienne (1984), *From Aristotle to Darwin and Back*, Notre Dame, IN: University of Notre Dame Press.

Goldman, Alvin (1986), *Epistemology and Cognition*, Cambridge, Mass: Harvard University Press.

Griffiths, Paul (1994), 'Why We Need Interreligious Polemics', *First Things*, June/July.

Haack, Susan (1993), *Evidence and Inquiry*, Cambridge: Blackwell.

Hales, Stephen (2006), *Relativism and the Foundations of Philosophy*, Cambridge, Mass: MIT Press.

Hamilton, William (1861), *The Metaphysics of Sir William Hamilton*, edited by Francis Bowen, Boston, Mass: Allyn and Bacon.

Harré, Rom and Krausz, Michael (1996), *Varieties of Relativism*, Oxford: Blackwell.

Harris, James (1992), *Against Relativism*, La Salle, Ill: Open Court.

Hill, Kevin (2007), *Nietzsche: A Guide for the Perplexed*, London: Continuum.

Hume, David (1965), *Of the Standard of Taste, and Other Essays*, edited by John W. Lenz, Indianapolis, Ind: Bobbs-Merrill.

Hyman, John (2004), 'Realism and Relativism in the Theory of Art', *Proceedings of the Aristotelian Society*, Vol. 105, No. 1, pp. 25–53.

Isaac, Jeffrey C. (1989), 'Review of *Whose Justice? Which Rationality?*', *Political Theory*, Vol. 17, No. 4, pp. 663–701.

James, William (1926), 'Letter to Dickinson S. Miller dated August 5, 1907', *The Letters of William James, Volume 2*, edited by Henry James, Boston, Mass: Little, Brown.

Jordan, James (1971), 'Protagoras and Relativism', *Southwestern Journal of Philosophy*, Vol. II, No. 3, pp. 7–29.

Kihlstrom, John (2004), 'Joseph Jastrow and His Duck – Or is it a Rabbit?', http://socrates.berkeley.edu/~kihlstrm/JastrowDuck.htm.

Kuhn, Thomas (1957), *The Copernican Revolution*, Cambridge, Mass: Harvard University Press.

—— (1977), *The Essential Tension*, Chicago, Ill:University of Chicago Press.

—— (1996), *The Structure of Scientific Revolutions*, 3rd edition, Chicago, Ill: University of Chicago Press.

Lacey, A. R. (1986), *A Dictionary of Philosophy*, London: Routledge.

Lewis, C. S. (2001), *The Abolition of Man*, San Francisco, Calif: Harper.

Lockie, Robert (2003), 'Relativism and Reflexivity', *International Journal of Philosophical Studies*, Vol. 11, pp. 319–39.

Luper, Steven (2004), 'Epistemic Relativism', *Epistemology: Philosophical Issues*, edited by Ernest Sosa and Enrique Villanueva, Oxford: Blackwell.

Lutz, Christopher (2004), *Tradition in the Ethics of Alasdair MacIntyre: Relativism, Thomism and Philosophy*, Oxford: Lexington Books.

MacDonald, George (1996), *Thomas Wingfold: Curate*, Whitehorn, Calif: Johannesen.

MacIntyre, Alasdair (1971), *Against the Self-Images of the Age*, New York, NY: Shoken.

—— (1982), 'Philosophy and its History', *Analyse & Kritik*, Vol. 4, pp. 102–13.

—— (1984), *After Virtue*, 2nd edition, Notre Dame, IN: University of Notre Dame Press.

—— (1988), *Whose Justice? Which Rationality?*, Notre Dame, IN: University of Notre Dame Press.

—— (1990), *Three Rival Versions of Moral Inquiry*, Notre Dame, IN: University of Notre Dame Press.

—— (1994), 'How Can We Learn What *Veritatis Splendor* Has To Teach?', *Thomist*, Vol. 58, No. 2, pp. 171–95.

Maimonides (1995), *Guide for the Perplexed*, Indianapolis, Ind: Hackett.

Margolis, Joseph (1987), 'Robust Relativism', *Philosophy Looks at the Arts*, 3rd edition, edited by Joseph Margolis, Philadelphia, Pa: Temple University Press.

Mill, John Stuart (1866), *An Examination of Sir William Hamilton's Philosophy*, Boston, Mass: W. V. Spencer.

Moser, Paul and Carson, Thomas (2000), *Moral Relativism: A Reader*, Cambridge: Cambridge University Press.

Mosteller, Timothy (2006a), *Relativism in Contemporary American Philosophy*, London: Continuum.

—— (2006b), 'Religious Epistemic Relativism', *Philosophia Christi*, Vol. 8, No. 1, pp. 65–84.

Nagel, Thomas (1997), *The Last Word*, Oxford: Oxford University Press.

Naugle, David (2003), *Worldview: The History of a Concept*, Grand Rapids, Mich: Eerdmans.

Newman, Andrew (2002), *The Correspondence Theory of Truth*, Cambridge: Cambridge University Press.

O'Grady, Paul (2002), *Relativism*, Montreal: McGill-Queen's University Press.

Phillips, Patrick (2007), *The Challenge of Relativism*, London: Continuum.

Plantinga, Alvin (1999), 'On Heresy, Mind and Truth', *Faith and Philosophy*, Vol. 16, No. 2, pp. 183–93.

Plato (1997), *Complete Works*, edited by John M. Cooper, Indianapolis, Ind: Hackett.

Pojman, Louis (1995), 'Relativism', *Cambridge Dictionary of Philosophy*, Cambridge: Cambridge University Press.

Putnam, Hilary (1981), 'Why Reason Can't Be Naturalized', *Realism and Reason: Philosophical Papers Volume III*, Cambridge: Cambridge University Press, 1983.

—— (1987), *The Many Faces of Realism*, La Salle, Ill: Open Court.

—— (1988), *Representation and Reality*, Cambridge, Mass: MIT Press.

—— (1992), *Renewing Philosophy*, Cambridge, Mass: Harvard University Press.

—— (1993), 'The Question of Realism', *Words and Life*, edited by James Conant, Cambridge, Mass: Harvard University Press, 1994.

—— (1994), 'Sense, Nonsense, and the Senses: An Inquiry into the Powers of the Human Mind', *Journal of Philosophy*, Vol. 91, No. 9, pp. 445–517.

—— (1996), 'What the spilled beans can spell: the difficult and deep realism of William James', *Times Literary Supplement*, 2 June, pp. 14–15.

—— (2004), *Ethics Without Ontology*, Cambridge, Mass: Harvard University Press.

Quine, W. V. O. (1969), *Ontological Relativity and Other Essays*, New York, NY: Columbia University Press.

Raatikainen, Panu (2001), 'Putnam, Languages and Worlds', *Dialectica*, Vol. 55, No. 1, pp. 167–74.

Rachels, James (2007), *The Elements of Morality*, 5th edition, Boston, Mass: McGraw Hill.

Ratzinger, Joseph (1996), 'Relativism: The Central Problem for the Faith Today', http://www.ewtn.com/library/CURIA/RATZRELA.HTM.

Rorty, Richard (1989), *Contingency, Irony, and Solidarity*, Cambridge: Cambridge University Press.

—— (1991), *Essays on Heidegger and Others*, Cambridge: Cambridge University Press.

Schiller, F. C. S. (1912), *Studies in Humanism*, 2nd edition, London: Macmillan.

Seung, T. K. (2007), *Kant: A Guide for the Perplexed*, London: Continuum.

Siegel, Harvey (1987), *Relativism Refuted: A Critique of Contemporary Epistemological Relativism*, Dordrecht: D. Reidel Publishing Company.

—— (2004), 'Relativism', *Handbook of Epistemology*, edited by Ilkka Niiniluoto, Matti Sintonen and Jan Wolenski, Dordrecht: Kluwer, pp. 747–80.

Sire, James (2004), *Naming the Elephant*, Downers Grove, Ill: InterVarsity Press.

Smith, R. Scott (2003), *Virtue Ethics and Moral Knowledge*, Aldershot: Ashgate.

Snider, Wric W. (1989), 'Review of *Whose Justice? Which Rationality?*', *Metaphilosophy*, Vol. 20, Nos. 3 and 4, pp. 387–90.

Solomon, Miriam (1990), 'On Putnam's Argument for the Inconsistency of Relativism', *Southern Journal of Philosophy*, Vol. XXVIII, No. 2, pp. 213–20.

Spencer, Herbert (1958), *First Principles*, New York, NY: De Witt.

Stump, Eleanor (1999), 'Orthodoxy and Heresy', *Faith and Philosophy*, Vol. 16, No. 2, pp. 147–63.

Throop, William and Doran, Katheryn (1991), 'Putnam's Realism and Relativity', *Erkenntnis*, Vol. 34, pp. 357–69.

Vico, Giambattista (1988), *On the Most Ancient Wisdom of the Italians*, translated by L. M. Palmer, Ithaca, NY: Cornell University Press.

Vinci, Thomas (1995), 'Solipsism', *Cambridge Dictionary of Philosophy*, Cambridge: Cambridge University Press.

Vision, Gerald (2004), *Veritas*, Cambridge, Mass: MIT Press.

Wallace, R. Jay (1989), 'Review of *After Virtue* and *Whose Justice? Which Rationality?*', *History and Theory*, Vol. XXVII, No. 3, pp. 326–48.

Weinstein, Jack Russell (2003), *On MacIntyre*, New York, NY: Wadsworth.

Willard, Dallas (1993), 'Predication as Originary Violence: A Phenomenological Critique of Derrida's View of Intentionality', edited by G. B. Madison, *Working Through Derrida*, Evanston, Ill: Northwestern University Press, pp. 120–36.

Williamson, Rene De Visme (1947), 'The Challenge of Political Relativism', *Journal of Politics*, Vol. 9, No. 2, pp. 147–77.

Windelband, Wilhelm (1901), *A History of Philosophy*, London: Macmillan.

Wittgenstein, Ludwig (1953), *Philosophical Investigations*, translated by G. E. M. Anscombe, New York, NY: Macmillan.

Young, James (1997), 'Relativism and the Evaluation of Art', *Journal of Aesthetic Education*, Vol. 31, No. 1, pp. 9–22.

Zellner, Harold (1995), 'Is Relativism Self-Defeating?', *Journal of Philosophical Research*, Vol. XX, pp. 287–95.

INDEX